ESSAYS ON TEACHING READING

Books by **Marlow Ediger** *and*
Digumarti Bhaskara Rao

Administration of Schools
Community Colleges
Curriculum Organisation
Curriculum of School Subjects
Effective Schooling
Effective School Curriculum
Elementary Curriculum
Elementary Curriculum Improvement
Essays on Teaching Mathematics
Essays on Teaching Science
Essays on Teaching Social Studies
Essays on Teaching Reading
Essays on Teaching and Learning
Improving School Administration
Issues in School Curriculum
Language Arts Curriculum
Philosophy and Curriculum
Psychology and Curriculum
Quality School Education
Reading Curriculum and Instruction
Relevancy in Elementary Curriculum
School Organisation
School Curriculum and Administration
Science Curriculum
Teaching English Successfully
Teaching Language Arts Successfully
Teaching Mathematics Successfully
Teaching Science Successfully
Teaching Social Studies Successfully
Teaching Mathematics in Elementary Schools
Teaching Science in Elementary Schools
Successful School Administration
Successful School Education

published by
Discovery Publishing House

ESSAYS ON TEACHING READING

by

Dr. Marlow Ediger
Emeritus Professor of Education
Truman State University
P.O. Box 417, 201 W 22nd St
North Newton KS 67117
United States of America

Dr. Digumarti Bhaskara Rao
Reader and Research Director
R.V.R. College of Education
D-43 (277) S.V.N. Colony
Guntur 522006, India

DISCOVERY PUBLISHING HOUSE PVT. LTD.
NEW DELHI-110 002

Published by:
Tilak Wasan
DISCOVERY PUBLISHING HOUSE PVT. LTD.
4831/24, Prahlad Street, Ansari Road
Darya Ganj, New Delhi-110002 (India)
Phone: +91-11-23279245, 43764432
Fax: +91-11-23253475
E-mail: parul.wasan@gmail.com
discoverypublishinghouse@gmail.com
info@discoverypublishinggroup.com
web: www.discoverypublishinggroup.com

***First Edition:* 2011**
ISBN: 978-81-8356-881-4

Essays on Teaching Reading

Printed at:
Shree Balaji Art Press
Delhi

dedicated
to

Chandra Sarat Chandra

Preface

Reading is a complex cognitive process of decoding symbols for the intention of deriving meaning and/or constructing meaning. It is the mastery of basic cognitive processes to the point where there is the analysis of meaning. It is a means of language acquisition, of communication, and of sharing information and ideas. It is a complex interaction between the text and the reader which is shaped by the reader's prior knowledge, experiences, attitude, and language community which is culturally and socially situated. The reading process requires continuous practices, development, and refinement. Readers use a variety of reading strategies to assist with decoding the written text and comprehension. Readers may use morpheme, semantics, syntax and context clues to identify the meaning of unknown words. Readers integrate the words they have read into their existing framework of knowledge. Now the teaching of reading is made a teaching component in many schools across the advanced countries.

In the successful teaching of reading, the teaching learning equipment, the teacher, the curriculum, the library, the language laboratory, the academic atmosphere, the teaching-learning programmes, etc., play their legitimate role.

This book will be of great use to curriculum designers and teachers and administrators.

Digumarti Bhaskara Rao
digumartibhaskararao@redeiffmail.com

Sri Sai Soudha
D-43 S.V.N. Colony
Guntur 522006
India

Contents

Contents

CHAPTER 1

Reading : For What Purposes?

When supervising university student teachers in the public schools, we asked the student teacher and cooperating teacher what the purpose was in a conducted reading lesson. Perplexed, the two teachers asked what I meant. We explained to both that they were to give reasons for teaching the lesson. They appeared to feel that it was quite obvious and the answer was "phonics". But, the question arose why phonics rather than a different skill was taught due to several pupils showing skill in phonetic analysis. Teachers need to be certain why selected subject matter, skills, or attitudes are being taught. Teaching reading needs to be purpose driven, not what is emphasized sequentially in a basal text or other source being used.

Purpose Driven Reading Instruction

Reading teachers need to stress what pupils *need* to become better readers. If selected learners are quite proficient in phonics to identify unknown words, then a different objective needs to be in evidence. We have observed a plethora of times in which a pupil reads fluently and yet beginning learnings in phonics are being taught in the classroom. Reading teachers need to make careful, recorded observations of what is necessary for learners individually to improve in reading. What each child needs becomes a purpose for reading instruction. Strategies may then be developed to achieve that goal. Reading instruction needs to be based on :

- one or more carefully thought through purposes per lesson
- readiness factors possessed by the learner whereby he/she will benefit optimally from the reading strategy being used
- meaning attached to each relevant fact, concept, and generalization
- interest to be developed within each pupil leading to active involvement within ongoing learning opportunities.

The reading teacher must review anecdotal, dated statements to ascertain *where* pupils are in achievement, at the present time, before teaching the ensuing lesson. By studying pupils present reading achievement, the reading teacher develops feelings of confidence in meeting personal needs of children. He/she bases decisions made on the best available information on which reading strategy to use in teaching. Thus, a strategy to follow must involve rational thought, critical and creative thinking. To blindly teach what pupils already know about syllabication, for example, wastes teaching time as well as learning time for pupils. The opposite might also occur whereby the reading teacher jumps too far ahead of learners when teaching reading. Thus, for example, in reading information text materials, there are too many new words encountered by pupils, even though these were introduced well prior to the reading experience. A very heavy vocabulary load then hinders pupils from understanding what was read and minimizes interest factors in reading expository content.

A quality lesson plan takes a plethora of variables into consideration. First, there needs to be strategy for motivating pupils for the ensuing lesson. The illustrations in the basal may be ample in number and possess clarity. Illustrations from the internet and World Wide Web might well provide subject-matter for additional discussion and elaboration. These need analyzing within a classroom environment which encourages active participation by learners. Hypotheses are freely developed in terms of what the story is about. The hypotheses may deal with one segment, for example, of narrative content such as characterization. Or additional elements may be added for hypotheses development such as the setting and plot of the narrative. As this is being done, the reading teacher may print the new words to be read in manuscript style for all pupils to see clearly. These may include vocabulary terms and need to be recognized and meaning attached to each as is used in the context of the narrative. Pupils with teacher guidance may check each hypothesis as the reading experience progresses. To maintain sequential ideas, words not recognized by learners should be pronounced by the teacher or another designated pupil. Each pupil's ideas must be respected regardless of the sincere quality of the hypothesis previously presented. In checking hypotheses, careful attention must be given to what the narrative author has written. An author's writing may be quite open-ended, leaving considerable leeway for interpretation. This provides opportunities for critical thinking when separating fact from opinion, as well as fantasy from reality. Creative thought, too, may be involved in that novel, unique ideas are presented. A rich discussion whereby learners truly assess hypotheses makes for a teaching strategy involving higher levels of cognition. Thinking skills are highly useful in school and in society. Follow-up experiences from silent/oral reading might include the following based on pupil developmental levels :

- developing a related mural which indicates salient concepts and generalizations.
- creatively dramatizing a segment or the entire narrative. Cooperative planning is needed to engage learners in different roles.
- doing a reader's theater whereby designated readers read their respective parts with voice inflection, proper stress, pitch, and juncture.

- reading/reporting to the class on a library book by the same author or on a similar topic.
- rewriting the character, the setting, or some other facet of the library book.

Pupils, as a result, should appreciate reading for a variety of purposes. Reading for enjoyment needs to be a by product of reading. The attitudes and feelings acquired should emphasize a desire to do more reading and a use for more intelligences such as the fine arts and its interrelationships with other academic areas and skills. Too frequently, pupils feel they are trapped in a teaching routine such round robin reading, and reading then has little to offer to accomplish, achieve, develop, and grow. Pupils need to have opportunities to look for new, fascinating procedures in teaching/learning situations involving reading. They should look forward to reading as a curriculum area. There are a plethora of procedures in reading instruction which include :

- individualized reading whereby pupils, informally, select a library book of their own choosing to read at a designated time during the school day.
- formation of a small friendship group which engages in an open ended discussion involving a self chosen book
- dyads organized to summarize ideas from reading an informational book
- a committee making sack puppets and a small stage to present content read from a basal reader
- pupil-teacher planning of an initiating or followup activity pertaining to a reading experience
- shared story time reading whereby the teacher reads aloud and then at flexible times discusses inherent content with learners
- pupils paraphrasing what was read as an evaluation of comprehension.

A relevant purpose in literature is to stress a variety of genre. Multicultural literature emphasizes pupils reading/

studying diverse cultures such as Latinos, African Americans, the Old Order Amish, Arab Americans, among others. Positive attitudes and acceptance need to be developed toward each. Visitors from the community of multicultural groups must be invited into the classroom to show products and artifacts. Processes may also be shared such as in native food preparation and art work. Pupils need to connect with other cultures, with culture to culture literature, and with the world. This will involve a series of sequential, rich endeavours over time. Authentic experiences need to be in the offing which provide realistic experiences for children. With fascinating interactions among learners and the teacher, high expectations, too, need to be in the offing. Both the teacher and pupils need to expect optimal progress for all. Very frequently, pupils may experience scaffolding whereby what appears to be too complex may be softened by ordered questions from the teacher in which pupils then arrive inductively with an appropriate response. Also, to provide structure pertaining to what was learned, the teacher may ask pupils which major idea was read in a given selection. This can be evaluated by the group with teacher assistance until agreement is reached. After a main idea has been agreed upon, then subordinate ideas follow subsequently. This procedure helps learners to arrive at main and subordinate content, realizing the former has more significance but is bolstered by the latter.

IN CLOSING

Purpose in reading is driven by what is poignant for pupils presently as well as in the future. Purposes need to include sequence in their order of teaching. The reading teacher must possess proper perspective in ascertaining what has use for pupils. In staying abreast of the latest trends in teaching reading and studying what each pupil needs to become a competent reader, the reading teacher can become proficient and effective as a professional guiding optimal progress of learners.

CHAPTER 2

Plans of Reading Instruction

There are a plethora of plans available to assist teachers in the teaching of reading. Each plan has strengths and will be discussed briefly. The reading teacher needs to study and appraise each plan with the intent of incorporating an improved procedure in teaching and learning situations. Pupils differ from each other in numerous ways and adequate provision must be made to assist each in achieving as well as possible.

The Teacher, Reading, and the Pupil

A big book procedure has many strengths. Here in a small group of six or seven learners, the teacher must have a large book for all to see clearly. The chosen library book should contain illustrations to assist in making the print more meaningful for pupils. Interest in reading materials is a prime factor in the selection of library books. The library book should also be on the understanding level of pupils and avoid overly complex or too simplistic reading materials. The teacher discusses the illustrations and reads aloud the content the first time and observes pupils to see they follow along with the printed words. Next, the pupils read aloud together with the teacher. In this way, pupils need not stumble on unknown words but may focus on interesting ideas instead. With the read aloud, pupils may develop a basic sight vocabulary. In the third oral reading, pupils may read independently. Involved learners can then read independently. Pupils might then discuss the contents for comprehension. There are basically no interruptions in hesitating or in failure to recognize unknown words. Interruptions when viewing unknown words hinder fluency in reading and a lack of skill in word identification.

The teacher may wish to bring in some phonics such as asking pupils the following :

- is there a word, for example which begins like "cat" in the read aloud?
- is there a word which ends like "dog"?
- which word rhymes with "pen"?

Each of the above may be printed on the white board as given by pupils. Activities such as these sharpen learner abilities to transfer word recognition skills to new situations (Ediger, 2008a).

Second, basal readers, published by a leading publishing company and adopted by the local school district, is another approach used in teaching reading. The accompanying Manual to the basal readers provides assistance to the teacher to determine objectives for pupil attainment, learning opportunities to achieve these objectives and appraisal techniques to evaluate learner progress. These three items in curriculum development may be modified in the teaching and learning process, as needed. Thus, basal readers may be used in a formal manner as prescribed in the Manual, or used flexibly as needed to provide for individual differences.

The stories have been chosen by specialists in the field of reading. The Manual section, too, has been developed by reading specialists. They will emphasize, among other things, phonics, word attack skills, and different comprehension strategies to use in teaching. The chosen stories may not reflect the interests of learners, but ways of motivating pupils to enjoy the diverse stories is stressed. The Manual section does provide assistance to teachers in teaching if used informally to provide for the needs of learners (McConachie *et al.*, 2006).

Third, programmed readers use a carefully structured sequence whereby pupils make few errors in reading. This is especially true if the programme has been field tested. Thus, in programed reading the sequence moves forward very slowly into gradually more complex learnings. Thus on the monitor, the pupil may read a sentence or more, for example, and then respond to a multiple choice test item to notice pupil understanding. The correct answer then is provided. If the pupil was correct in responding, he/she is rewarded. If incorrect, the pupil still will go in to the next programmed item. Read, respond, check is used consistently in having pupils move forward in programmed. Programmers write the complete program of reading instruction which consists of objectives, programmed learning opportunities, and appraisal techniques consisting of answers to each item (Liang and Dole, 2006).

A fourth instructional plan involves individualized reading. A set of quality library books is placed at a centre for pupils to browse through and then each chooses a book to read. The individual pupil will choose a book of personal interest to read. He/she completes reading the entire book and then has a conference with the teacher. At the conference, comprehension will be evaluated through a discussion of library book content. The pupils is asked to read a selection from the library book to appraise fluency in reading. Notes are written and dated in order to refer to for the next conference when a completed library book has been read. Progress may be noted when making comparisons in pupil progress (Carlsen and Sherill, 1988).

Fifth, peer reading involves three or four peers taking turns reading aloud a chosen book. Guidelines are adhered to in cooperative learning endeavours. Assistance is provided in reading by peers as needed. A discussion follows of the content read with higher levels of cognition stressed. The teacher supervises the discussion. Peer teaching may be emphasized to assist in word recognition as well as in comprehension strategies. Independence in reading is stressed in small groups achieving objectives of instruction. For all reading experiences, pupils my extend learnings through a variety of activities such as creative dramatics (Bolton and Heathcote, 1995).

Sixth, after initial learnings have been achieved as in phonics and word recognition together with a basic sight vocabulary, linguistic procedures might be stressed in teaching pupils to advance in reading. It then is not necessary to view each word analytically, but the context of the reading material keeps the reader on track. Thus with sequentially reading a selection, the pupil will notice if he/she is or is not comprehending ideas contextually. A good reader then reads fluently and notices if he/she is on track. If the reader has strayed a little from the ideas presented by the writer, sequential ideas will lead to a corrected course (Goodman, 1996).

Seventh, the experience chart approach stresses a concrete/semi-concrete to abstract order of experiences. Thus, a set of pupils, for example, view and discuss a set of objects on an interest centre. In sequence, the learners provide information, orally, on what was observed for the teacher to record on a chalkboard as the sentences are given. As each sentence is given slowly, pupils see talk written down. Pupils then with teacher guidance read aloud the entire printed content as the teacher points to each word in sequence. Pupils may reread the content until mastered or before interest wanes. Here, pupils do not face difficulties in wgrd recognition. The teacher together with pupils read the subject matter aloud, followed by learners independently doing the reading as the teacher points to each word while it is being read. Ideas read are meaningful since pupils observed and discussed real objects, previously, at a learning center. This is a cooperative endeavor since pupils and the teacher worked together, harmoniously, to develop the experience chart (Ediger, 2006).

Eighth, a patterns approach is stressed in spelling which has tremendous implications for reading instruction. Thus in a basal spelling textbook, words for pupil mastery in a lesson, for example, might consist of the "man" pattern of words in a family: ban, can, fan, pan, among others. By changing an initial consonant in this case, pupils come up with a new word. Other word patterns may include the following :

- words ending in the suffix "ing"
- words containing a prefix, e.g. "un"
- words beginning with a selected letter, e.g. "l" as in lion, lamb, lonesome.
- words ending with a certain letter, such as "p," as in the words mop, pop, top.
- shorter words being inherent in longer words.

By noticing patterns in spelling words, pupils posses clues in word recognition. Certain patterns are repetitive and transfer to the identification of other words (Ediger 2008b).

Ninth, sustained silent reading (SSR) is a plan of reading whereby the pupil chooses a library book of his own liking to read silently. A special time is devoted during the school day for SSR. Pupils tend to select books on their own individual reading level so that meaning is attached to the activity. They also tend to choose library books of personal interest and worth. The purpose of SSR is to encourage reading time. Learners then practice the act of reading independently. The teacher monitors SSR to make sure that each child has selected a library book and is actively involved in reading. Generally, there is no direct teaching and no formal evaluation of reading progress here, except that the teacher observes involved pupils being actively involved in silent reading. The SSR does give pupils time to engage in decision making and taking responsibility for reading.

Tenth, the Great Books organization has much to offer pupils. Initially, the Great Books organization stressed the importance of pupils reading and enjoying the classics. Classical literature, in many cases, is too complex for elementary and middle school students. However, *Classics Illustrated,* for example, written in comic book form simplified the content of the Great Books. With large pictures and simplified accompanying print, many pupils tended to enjoy reading the content pertaining to Tom Sawyer, Huckleberry Finn, the House of Seven Gables, among others. Looking at the opposite side of the coin, there are experts who recommend that the classics be read in their original form at the high school and university level. The Great Books presently recommends that a class of pupils with teacher guidance choose a well written library book on the developmental level of children and cooperatively explore its contents in a stimulating manner. The purpose here is for pupils to read and enjoy good literature.

IN CONCLUSION

There are a plethora of plans in the teaching of reading. Each has its own unique appeal. Teachers and school administrators need to study indepth each plan and come up with the best in aiding pupils to achieve in reading. Perhaps, with a combination of ideas from the diverse plans, pupils may be assisted to gain in reading skills and thus increase comprehension to include critical and creative thinking, as well s problem solving skills.

References

Bolton, G., and D. Hearthecote (1995), *Drama for Learning.* Portsmouth, New Hampshire; Heinemann.

Carlsen, G. R., and A. Sherrill (1988), *Readers: How We Come to Love Books*. Urbana, Illinois: National Council Teachers of English.

Ediger, Marlow (2006), "Administration of Schools," *College Student Journal,* 40(4), 846-851.

Ediger, Marlow (2008a),"Psychology of Parental Involvement in Reading," *Reading Improvement*, 45 (1), 46-52.

Ediger, Marlow (2008b), "The Principal in the Teaching and Learning Process," *Education,* 129 (4), 574-578.

Goodman, Y. (1996), "Reevaluating Readers While Readers Revalue Themselves; Retrospective Miscue Analyses," *The Reading Teacher*, 19 (8), 600-615.

Liang, Lauren Aimonette, and Janice Dole (2006), "Help with Teaching Reading Comprehension: Comprehending Instructional Frameworks," *The Reading Teacher,* 59 (8).

McConachie (2006), "Task, Text, and Talk : Literacy for all Subjects," *Educational Leadership,* 64 (2), 8-15.

CHAPTER 3

Which Plan of Reading Instruction is the Best?

Which is the very best plan of reading instruction? There are a plethora of plans available to assist pupils to achieve more optimally. A major problem is to match the reading plan with the learner. Pupils need to accept and benefit from the chosen procedure. One size does not fit all; this expression has been used numerous times in referring to No Child Left Behind (NCLB) and is applicable to choosing a reading program for children. The question arises, "Which plan assists pupils to best become fluent readers?"

Different Philosophies of Reading Instruction

Each recommended plan of teaching and learning has selected key beliefs. The beliefs must translate into effective programs of teaching reading. Pupils need assistance to become good readers in decoding as well as in comprehension. The chosen plan of reading needs to harmonize with the possessed learning style (Ediger 2005):

- individualized reading stresses the pupil selecting which sequential library books to complete. Selections are based on learner interests with teacher/pupil conferences generally held after each completed book in reading. The selection of library books must be broad in genre and reading levels. What are the advantages of individualized reading?

1. decision-making is being emphasized by pupils. Decision-making is highly salient in school and in society.
2. to own the curriculum, pupils do better if choices are permitted in terms of what to read.
3. teachers must have a good knowledge of children's library books in order to stress quality in conferences with pupils. Pupils are to indicate decoding and comprehension skills.
4. time on task is important since pupils enjoy considerable freedom in choices made.

Disadvantages include the following :

1. selected pupils are not ready to choose a library book to read nor in settling down to read.
2. there are pupils who are hierarchical and want the teacher to make the choices.
3. certain teachers find it difficult in being adequately knowledgeable about children's literature in order to cary out quality discussions of children's literature in conference settings with pupils.
4. self discipline is difficult for the pupil in monitoring his/her own reading.

To every action, there is a somewhat equal reaction in choosing a plan of reading instruction. There are advantages and disadvantages for each. The plan adopted, in whole or in part, must meet personal needs of the individual and encourage interest in reading. Too frequently with drill and practice, interest is minimized. Much criticism has been aimed at mandated testing due to much repetitive teaching of possible skills on that test.

Basal readers have been popular over the years in teaching reading. The accompanying manual lists suggested objectives for pupil achievement, learning activities to achieve objectives, and evaluation procedures to achieve progress. The teacher may be creative in using the basal by considering it as a handbook, from which choices may be made in terms, for example, of learning activities (Fountas and Pinnell 1999).

For the teacher, there are suggestions for teaching in the Manual. This provides a richer repertoire in curriculum development, as well as in reading instruction. The pros in using basal readers also include the following :

1. beginning teachers, in particular, have security in teaching reading with the utilization of a carefully chosen basal and the accompanying Manual.
2. they are written and developed by specialists in the teaching of reading.

There are always disadvantages for any plan of teaching:

1. basals have not met the needs of selected pupils when providing for individual differences.
2. it becomes very formal and artificial when teachers become dependent on the Manual. Authentic teaching is then lacking.

Reading teachers must adapt instruction to individual learner needs, not what a manual may say or what other reading programs advocate. The focal point is the pupil and his/her need to become proficient in reading. When being a good reader, the pupil is able to read subject-matter in the natural sciences, the social sciences, the arts, as well as content in mathematics and the other academic disciplines. The pupil needs to make sequential progress with good teaching. A developmental program of instruction is then in evidence with room for the zone of proximal development (ZPD). The ZPD emphasizes where a pupil is presently in achievement with the reading teacher stressing a higher, possible achievable objective. That gap may be filled with quality learning activities. An issue in reading instruction pertains to a strong programme of phonics for young school aged children versus a whole language approach. Phonics instruction is of value when integrated with meaning in comprehension. There are consistent phonic understandings when relating specific graphemes and phonemes. Many a times, the reader identifies an unknown word through recognizing an initial consonant and utilizing context clues. Additional means of phonic word recognition include :

- dividing an unknown into syllables
- dividing an unknown into shorter words (Callow, 2008).

A Big Book approach in reading instruction might well emphasize a whole language approach in teaching reading. Thus, five to six pupil are seated around a large, interesting library book. The contents need to be clearly visible to those involved. A computer with a large screen may also be used. The teacher stimulates interest in reading by discussing the related illustrations with pupils. This is followed by the reading teacher pointing to each word read aloud, as pupils follow along carefully. The teacher needs to observe if each pupil is looking at sequential words intensively. The read aloud continues with pupils joining in. The activity may be repeated as often as desired.

Selected teachers bring in phonic learnings with asking questions such as the following :

- which words, for example, did we read which rhyme with "man?"
- which word(s) begin with the letter "d" as in dog?" (Lower case "d" and "dog" are printed on the board (Ediger 2003).

Phonic approaches should be taught based on individual pupil need. If a pupil knows selected phonic learnings, they must not be "taught" these same learnings again. When supervising university student teachers, the writer noticed that lesson plans incorporated phonics even though these had been mastered by selected pupils. Ensuing reading objectives should be new and challenging. A workable strategy needs to be utilized to assist pupils to attain relevant learnings. Diversity of purposeful experiences must be provide for remedial and developmental teaching.

Achieving measurably stated objectives versus open ended goals has drawn much attention in reading instruction. Presently, measurably stated objectives is receiving emphasis. No Child Left Behind (NCLB) has emphasized testing to challenge and motivate learners to work harder. The NCLB is being revised and, no doubt, will stress nationwide testing. Test results are precise and provide a number such as a percentile, or grade equivalent. This provides data for failing or promoting a pupil in moving on to the next grade level. There are a plethora of difficulties involved in having pupils take a single standardized test to notice achievement, progress, and promotional purposes (Campbell, 2007). These include the following :

- generally, multiple choice test items are used and pupils are to choose the "correct" response whereby the response may not be that clear cut.
- higher levels of cognition are minimized since "correctness," as defined by test writers, is being stressed in choosing the right answer.
- thinking outside the box is definitely discouraged. Thus, creative and critical thinking, as well as problem are greatly minimized.
- test writers, unknown to teachers and pupils, come from areas removed from the local school. This would not square with constructivism, a psychology of learning, or that the teacher needs to know pupils well and their individual capabilities to teach reading effectively.
- vast numbers of tests are machine scored and thus uniformity is emphasized in time limits for test taking,

the same test items for each grade level of pupils taking the test, and the same norms for evaluating each pupil's score on the test.

Standardized tests attempt to have "sameness" in all its contents and methods of test taking, but the major difference is that pupils differ from each other in myriad ways. Education should not standardize pupils, but be modified to provide for different interests, and abilities of learners. Pupils progress at diverse rates of speed and have different goals in life. When looking at all the listed occupations of workers in a nation, individuals truly have many choices and decisions to make. These should be made on the basis of the learner's talents and what he/she can do well with involved purposes. High school students must be assisted to make personal choices based on what is perceived salient by the student. Forcing the student to make occupational and vocational choices is to be frowned upon. Dogmatic advice also is abhorrent. Student need to be respected and valued for their own sake. Rudeness and intimidation have no roles to play in teaching, learning, and guidance services. Students are human beings with feelings, values, and attitudes. Attitudes need to be accepting of others, respectful, and polite (Bottoms 2008).

REFERENCES

Bottoms, Gene (2007), "Treat all Students Like the "Best" Students," *Educational Leadership*, 64 (7), 30-32.

Callow, Jon (2008), "Show Me: Principles for Assessing Student's Visual Literacy," *The Reading Teacher*, 61 (8), 616-628.

Campbell, Peter (2007), Edison is the Symptom, NCLB is the Disease," *Phi Delta Kappan*, 438-443.

Ediger, Marlow (2003), *Teaching Reading Successfully*. New Delhi, India: Discovery Publishing House.

Ediger, Marlow (2005), *Philosophy of Education*. New Delhi, India: Discovery Publishing House.

Fountas, I. C., and G. S. Pinnell (1999), *Matching Books to Readers: Using Leveled Books in Guided Reading, K-3*, Portsmith, New Hampshire: Heinemann.

CHAPTER 4

Shared Reading, the Pupil and the Teacher

Pupil-teacher interaction provides opportunities for many kinds of learning experiences. Within the reading curriculum, there are a plethora of activities in oral communication and working together harmoniously. Thus from every day experiences, the teacher may communicate verbally what he/she has read in an interesting, informative manner on the pupil's developmental level. This broadens the knowledge repertoire of children in the classroom. Pupils, too, may share content read with others learners. Ongoing standards might well be developed in sharing ideas gleaned from reading. Teachers need to be on the lookout for materials in securing and maintaining pupil interest in shared reading.

Procedures to Use in Shared Reading

The big book approach provides opportunities for pupils to engage in shared reading. The library book needs to be large enough for a small group of pupils to be able to see the print clearly from where they are seated comfortably. Learners with teacher assistance might then view and discuss the illustrations therein. Pupil comments and interaction is salient. Engaging pupil curiosity in the illustrations and story content is important. An appreciation for children's literature should always be a major objective in shared reading.

After readiness has been provided, pupils need to follow along in the print as the teacher reads the script aloud, pointing to each word being read. The teacher serves as a model in reading enthusiastically. Pupils may then notice meaningful words in context. Next, pupils need to read aloud together with the teacher as the shared reading experience continues. Questions from pupils are invited to stimulate interest in literature. The reading activity may be repeated as often as desired with the read aloud, followed by pupils doing the oral reading. Learning to read is being emphasized within the shared reading experience, using the big book approach (Ediger and Rao, 2005).

Pupils do not stumble over unknown words nor feel embarrassed due to lacking specific reading skills. Liking reading as a satisfying activity is being promoted. The big book approach may also be used with struggling readers in different grade levels.

As a second activity, many pupils enjoy doing an experience chart collectively. Objects may be placed on an interest centre whereby learners look at each and discuss fascinating features among themselves and the teacher as a shared oral communication activity. The richness in these experiences comes about due to pupils viewing and manipulating concrete items; authenticity is involved when life like learnings are in evidence. The teacher assists in helping pupils to attach meaning to each item at the interest center by raising purposeful questions and encouraging thinking.

Pupils are asked to present ideas on what was observed and this is teacher recorded in neat manuscript letters on the chalkboard or with the use of an overhead projector. The teacher models the oral reading activity as pupils observe the printed words. Pupils may read their very own ideas together with the teacher as the latter points to each sequential word. This activity interests many pupils and presents a quality model in learning to read. Children do like to hear and read the same content over again with the teacher and then by themselves. Sharing ideas in developing the experience chart and adding or deleting content may also be stressed (McGee and Schickedanz, 2007). The writer when supervising university student teachers has observed the experience chart concept be used on different grade levels and also in remedial reading. Other objects as well as illustrations might be used, too, for future experience charts. The charts should be saved for rereading at later times.

The writer, too, has noticed when supervising university student teachers how carefully pupils listen to the teacher reading a library book aloud and then stopping at a given point and having learners predict what will happen next. Predictions may be typed into a word processor and shown in large letters on an attached screen for all pupils to see clearly. The predictions may be checked with the teacher reading sequentially from the library book. Here, pupils focus on story sense. Predictions may also be made by pupils on the kind of character, setting, and plot of story content. Predictions become hypotheses to be checked. This provides opportunities for indepth discussions. Pupils cooperatively may develop a different setting for a story and then discuss how this might alter the character or plot (Tichman, 2008).

Pupils tend to enjoy echoic reading activities. Here, the teacher reads a selection from a trade book which lends itself to pupils repeating orally a part read aloud by the teacher. Voice inflection is important with proper stress, pitch, and pauses, to convey meaning as an echo. The selection chosen by the teacher needs to be on the understanding and interest level of pupils. Not only is appropriate prosody emphasized, but also content as well as attitudes toward reading. Vocabulary development through contextual learnings, too, may be achieved. The teacher needs to clearly model an echoic reading activity with learners realizing this is a shared experience. Cooperation is necessary in order to read together the echoic part. When supervising university student teachers, the writer has observed numerous teaching situations whereby echoic reading was used and pupil attention was thoroughly grounded in this experience (Ortlieb *et al.* 2007).

Rhymed verse lends itself to sharing all or part of a selection. Rhymed verse may also be composed by pupils individually or collectively. Many teachers, too, have written verse which contains rhyme and is then shared with pupils. A good teachers anthology of poetry provides excellent models for rhyme in poetry (Walter, 1982). The following kinds of rhymed verse tend to promote much enthusiasm among pupils :

- couplets whereby two lines are written with ending words rhyming. Mother Goose contains many favourite rhyming poems for pupil enjoyment, such as Jack and the Candlestick :

  Jack be nimble, Jack be quick

  Jack jumped over the candlestick

- triplets with three lines and all ending words rhyme. The following was written by a committee of pupils in an ongoing unit of study and read collectively with blended voices :

  Hail

  The spring weather was quite pleasant

  Followed by a cooling down of each plant

  With pieces of ice from the sky falling at a slant

- quatrains with all four lines ending with rhyme. The following quatrain was written by a fifth grader and shared with others :

  Erosion

  With no cover crop for the moisture to hold

  A very heavy rain caused soil to erode

Trees and grass might have slowed the runoff bold
Wasted top soil hinders production of future crops sold.

- limericks with lines one, two, and five rhyming as well as lines three and four containing rhyme.

By writing/reading poetry, orally and cooperatively, pupils hear patterns of rhyme, voice inflection, and become increasingly proficient in noticing grapheme/phoneme correspondence, as well as diverse kinds of poetry which might well expand into free verse, haiku, tankas, diamantes, and septolets, among others. Reading and writing haiku, for example, assist pupils to recognize a certain number of syllables, such as five, seven, five, for each of three lines respectively.

Dividing a story or expository selection into play parts whereby several pupils may practice and read/recite their individual selection can make for quality sharing of literature. Selecting the narrative for writing play parts emphasizes cooperation and respect for each other. Pupils need to work together for the good of all in the presentation. Once parts are assigned/volunteered for, learners might then read and reread parts until suitable for presentation in the classroom. They may be memorized if desired or read aloud. Prosody is very salient here in that the feeling dimension of each person is expressed within his/her play part. The writer has also noticed where pupils wrote their very own play on the sixth grade level. There is considerable satisfaction involved when readiness exists for writing a play creatively. There also are feelings of reward when a play is used directly from a basal reader.

Writing play parts from an expository account in a historical unit being studied, for example, provides challenges for many learners in the upper grades. Pupils can truly become wholeheartedly involved in this activity. The expository writing, then, needs to be rewritten and divided into parts for readers to present in its final form. The rewards are great for pupils in these kinds of writing activities and intrinsically satisfying. The teacher has very important responsibilities here when monitoring and assisting pupils in writing and in oral communication experiences. There is much emphasis placed upon shared reading when planning and reading aloud the different play parts.

As another example of shared reading, choral reading emphasizes pupils and teachers working together in the curriculum. Here, the teacher reads orally a part of a selection which has a refrain. After the read aloud by the teacher, pupils cooperatively read aloud the refrain. Quality oral reading by the teacher together with pupil blended voices for the refrain might well be a very rewarding experience for learners. There appears to be a pattern with the teacher's role and the pupils response in shared reading activities (Tiedt, 1982).

CONCLUSION

Shared reading offers pupils variety in experiences whereby pupils success is involved. Thus, pupils need not feel embarrassed by stumbling over unknown words. In most situations, they read aloud together with the teacher and other learners as in the big book approach. Here, pupils develop a basic sight vocabulary as well as read fluently. Success tends to improve the self concept, as well as feeling confident in learning. Each experience discussed helps pupils to enjoy reading. Literature used in reading needs to possess interest which should propel learners to pursue a variety of genres in trade books, among other sources. Pupil purpose in learning increases with the interest factor involved. The teacher serves as a role model in assisting pupils to enjoy literature. Meaningful experiences accumulate as pupils engage in different kinds of shared reading approaches.

REFERENCES

Ediger, Marlow, and D. Bhaskara Rao (2005), *Language Arts Curriculum*. New Delhi, India : Discovery Publishing House.

McGee, Lea M., and Judith A. Schickedanz 2007), "Repeated Interactive Read Alouds in Preschool and Kindergarten," *The Reading Teacher*, 60 (8), 742-751.

Ortleib, Evan, et.al. (2007), "The Art of Reading: Dramatizing Literacy," *Reading Improvement*, 44 (3), 169-176.

Tichman, Sheri (2008), "The Object of Their Attention," *Educational Leadership*, 65 (5), 44-47.

Tiedt, Iris M. (1982), *The Language Arts Handbook*. Englewood Cliffs, New Jersey: Prentice Hall, Inc.

Walter, Nina (1982), *Let Them Write Poetry*. New York; Holt Rinehart and winston.

CHAPTER 5

For an Effective Reading Programme

An effective programme of reading instruction must meet the needs of pupils individually. Pupils in a classroom differ from each other on present reading achievement levels. They also come to the classroom with diverse abilities, interests, and attitudes toward reading and literacy in general. Thus, the reading teacher must consider a plethora of factors when assisting learners in the teaching of literacy. What makes for a quality program of instruction?

Quality in the Reading Curriculum

Teachers and supervisors need to plan a reading program which motivates pupils. The content should contain literature which is of interest to learners. Pupils may then be observed in being actively engaged in reading. The teacher must provide readiness experiences prior to pupils being involved in the reading process. Readiness emphasizes motivated pupils who benefit from the ensuing activity. Stimulating questions pertaining to the new content needs to be in the offing. If basals are used, the illustrations therein provide readiness ideas for a discussion of related subject matter. From the discussion, pupils raise questions which they would like to have answered. Reading the ensuing content might well provide those answers. Prior to the reading experience, pupils need to be introduced to possible new words to be read. These may be highlighted by being shown on the computer screen or by using the overhead projector. The teacher needs to be certain that pupils can identify these words while reading and understand their contextual meaning. With interesting methods used to identify questions as well as present the new words in context, pupils should feel motivated to read the ensuing lesson. Exciting discussions tend to follow (Ediger and Rao, 2007).

Second, adopted reading programmes should be based on a firm research and theoretical base. Outdated ideas and opinions need to be discarded. Meaning theory of reading instruction should be emphasized. Learners need to understand content in literary selections. Meaning attached to the setting, characterization, plot, irony, and theme make for eager learners wanting to do more reading of narrative content. Expository subject matter can make for equal enthusiasm in its reading. Answering questions pertaining to different facets of content increases interest. Children love to speculate on literary elements pertaining to "What if", questions. They like to scaffold ideas based on stimulating points of view presented. Indepth meanings might then well accrue (Ediger, 2007).

A favourable classroom climate needs to be promoted to help learners achieve more optimally. The reasons why teachers like to control students instead of managing them are :

- They are socialized to believe or are instructed that the marks of a good teacher is to have control over the class.
- The amount of control teachers have in the class is often seen by the administrator as a measure of the quality of a teacher.

- They are afraid of losing control if students have increased autonomy.
- They fear that students with with less control will not want to learn what the teacher wants to teach (Bindhu, 2008).

Teachers and school administrators need to promote a classroom climate which is conduce to pupil learning. A relaxed, studious atmosphere must prevail. Pupils should like school and the different curriculum areas taught. If pupils do not care for education and schooling, reasons for this occurring must be diagnosed. Pleasant school surroundings need to replace that which is negative. The next standard might, in part, help to make for needed change in the curriculum.

Third, pupils should choose reading materials from a wide variety of fascinating library books. Thus, from a variety of topics and genres on display in the classroom, the learner may choose an interesting library book to read. Pupils need to have ample opportunities to make choices and decisions, from among alternatives. The choices stress choosing a library book, among others, to read sequentially, during time devoted to individualized reading. The teacher needs to assist pupils to choose sequential library books for silent reading who initially cannot settle down to select and read a library book. The teacher needs to observe which pupils are/are not actively engaged in individualized reading. Self selection of reading materials encourages skills in decision making and promotes pupil responsibility in making choices (McConachie *et al.*, 2006).

Creativity is a key goal in literacy. The pupil needs encouragement to read creatively. Unique interpretations of what has been read is salient. Individual or collective creativity in responses are important. Originality of interpretation may be shown through :

- art products such as drawings, pencil sketching, mural development, and water color products
- construction experiences including making models, paper mache' items, and puppets

- poetry writing such as haiku, tankas, quatrains, limericks, and free verse
- dramatic experiences including pantomimes, and creative dramatizations (Tiedt, 1982).

Novel works should always be encouraged from and through a variety of reading experiences. They may well be means of indicating comprehension from reading and discussions.

Different genres must be available for pupil selection of reading materials. Pupils possess unique interests in subject-matter content. Attractive books, readily available, should be checked out with ease. These books may be introduced by the teacher and/or the school librarian. Introduced books need to be shown to students with a stimulating, short introduction read aloud. Selected library books may also be read aloud to students during story time. Voice inflection with proper stress, enunciation, and pitch assist in drawing learner attention to the contents during the read aloud.

The teacher as well as with student involvement need to develop attractive bulletin boards involving one or more new library books. The display needs to capture student attention. Book jackets of newly purchased library books, pictures of authors, and illustrations pertaining to these library books must be in the offing. Introduction of each subsequent bulletin board display should assist learners to do more reading of quality literature. A concerted effort should be made to encourage more learner reading. If library books are read sequentially, this will assist pupils to become increasingly proficient in reading. Reading needs to be an enjoyable activity. Of all skills possessed by the writer, reading would come first in importance. This does not minimize different academic areas since much reading is required to learn and achieve in each academic discipline. The act of reading is a skill and that skill is used to gather information for course work, the work place as well as for enjoyment. Each academic area also has its own requirements such as experimentation in the science curriculum. Reading of subject-matter, for example, relates well to doing experiments and further indepth studies in science. Reading is equally salient in doing word problems in mathematics and attaching meaning to mathematical symbols. In the social sciences, pupils need to become proficient in reading primary and secondary sources of information.

A quality library book reading programme will assist pupils to do more reading be it expository, narrative, and/or creative content such as poetry. What is read needs to be assessed. This goes beyond securing ideas literally from the selection(s) read. Critical reading stresses separating facts from opinions, fantasy from reality, as well as accurate from inaccurate content. Concepts and generalizations might then be realized from the synthesis.

Aesthetic reading stresses that pupils individually react and interpret content, based on previous experiences. Cai (2008) wrote the following :

> Aesthetic reading is personal, but is not simply identifying with characters or expressing personal likes and dislikes about the story, as is frequently misinterpreted. Aesthetic reading is a rather complicated process that includes evocation and responses.

Cai goes on to quote Rosenblatt (1982) pertaining to aesthetic reading:

> In aesthetic reading, we respond to the very story or poem we are evoking during the transaction with the text. In order to shape the work, we draw on our past reservoir of past experiences with people and the world, our past inner linkage of words and things, our past encounters with spoken or written texts. We listen to the sound of words in the inner ear; we lend our sensations, our emotions, our sense of being alive, to the new experience which we feel, corresponds to the to the text. We participate in the story, we identify with characters, we share their conflicts and their feelings. At the same time, there is a stream of responses being generalized. There may be a sense of pleasure in our own creative activity,

an awareness of pleasant or awkward sound and movement in the words, a feeling of approval or disapproval of the characters and their behavior.

Critical reading may follow with analyzing and value judgments made. Standards are used in making the evaluative statements. Students need to demonstrate individual reading successes in the following ways :

- using teacher observation in terms of recommended criteria
- evaluating the self in individual and cooperative learning endeavors
- results from teacher written tests such as essay and multiple choice items
- assessing art, dramatic, and written products of learners directly related to literacy content read (Ediger, 2008).

References

Bindhu, T. S. (2008), "Dynamics of Classroom Management," *Edutracks*,7 (10), 15-17. Published in India.

Cai, Mingshui (2008), "Transactional Theory and the Study of Multicultural Literature," *Language Arts*, 85 (3), 215.

Ediger, Marlow (2007), "The Substitute Teacher in Reading Instruction, *SubJournal*, 8 (2), 67-73.

Ediger, Marlow (2008), "Philosophy of Testing, Measurement, and Evaluation," *Edutracks*, 7 (10), 25-26.

Ediger, Marlow, and D. Bhaskara Rao (2007), Reading Curriculum and Instruction. New Delhi, India: Discovery Publishing House.

McConachie, et. al. (2006), "Task, Text, and Talk, Literacy for All Subjects," *Educational Leadership*, 64 (2), 8-15.

Rosenblatt, Louise (1982), "The Literary Transaction: Evocation and Response," *Theory into Practice*, 21 (4), 268-277.

Tiedt, Iris M. (1982), *The Language Arts Handbook*. Englewood Cliffs, New Jersey: Prentice Hall, Inc.

CHAPTER 6

High School Principal and Reading Across Curriculum

How many high school students do poorly in an academic area due to problems in reading comprehension? Secondary school teachers need to assess if this is a difficulty faced by students. Too frequently, it is assumed that elementary school teachers need to teach students how to read. But, there may be older students who did not learn read due to various reasons. These reasons may include the following :

- growing up in poverty with very limited reading materials in the home setting.
- models for motivation in reading were lacking in the home community.
- education was not perceived as being worthwhile or was even frowned upon.
- opportunities to learn were indeed limited.
- health problems, serous enough to preclude reading achievement and academic progress.

What Might the Principal Do To Assist in Reading Progress?

The high school principal needs to encourage teachers to ascertain if reading problems exist among students which hinder achievement. Teachers may have students read aloud in class a given assignment which requires reading. This needs to be done only one time generally, during a semester or school year. The read aloud should occur toward the beginning of the new school year. Approximately, 100 running words may be marked by the teacher for each student to read. The textbook should be read by identifying words correctly with approximately 88 to 95 per cent accuracy to be on the reading level of the involved student. Below the 88 per cent level, most readers have difficulty decoding an adequate number of words for comprehension purposes. To evaluate comprehension, the reader should be able to answer three of four questions asked, covering the content read. The teacher may record the kinds of errors made by each student. These usually may be categorized as in the following :

- substituting words for those in context
- hesitating five seconds, as a minimum, before the teacher pronounces that word
- repeating a word or phrase before proceeding with the ensuing selection
- skipping words
- mispronouncing words (Edtger and Rao, 2007).

Fluency in reading assists in comprehension of ideas. From the oral reading activity, the teacher may notice the kinds of help which students need to comprehend ideas more effectively. Assistance may be given in the following areas of decoding :

- phonics in which words or parts of words are consistently spelled between grapheme and phoneme.
- context clues whereby a word substituted by the student for the unknown makes sense within the sentence.

- picture clues used in the textbook to aid in word identification.

It may benefit students for the teacher to introduce new words appearing in the ensuing reading activity. These words must be printed in neat manuscript style on the chalkboard and discussed with students. Words printed here should be noticed carefully by learners so that they can be recognized in silent/oral reading. The meaning of each word as used in the textbook reading assignment must become part of the student repertoire.

Questions, too, may be written on the chalkboard to guide student comprehension when reading silently. These questions may be answered from the subject matter read in the reading assignment. It is appropriate for the teacher to read key ideas aloud to the class during the discussion. Students must become independent readers, but, in the meantime assistance needs to be given as needed. The assistance given aids students to learn to recognize words and comprehend what was read (Ediger, 2006).

Answers to questions discussed, following the silent reading, need to be relevant, useful, and seek student engagement Those who are turned off need motivation through a stimulating discussion with each student actively involved. Discussions may involve literal interpretation of content read. However, higher levels of thinking skills (HOTS), must be in the offing. Meaningful learnings always need to be pursued whereby the learner understands what is being discussed. Beyond literal interpretation, students need to engage in analytical thought, here, students with teacher guidance separate fact from opinion, fantasy from reality, and accurate from inaccurate statements. With analysis, learners separate ideas into component parts. This facet of learning fascinates many students. Students then are motivated in achieving and growing. The social facets of learning also need to be emphasized. Thus, standards of interaction among participants include respect for the thinking of others, treating each other humanely, as well encouraging active participation with quality ideas. Ridiculing and rudeness must be eliminated from discussion settings. They hinder student achievement and progress for both the perpetrators and receivers of comments. Positive interactions must be in the offing (Reis and Fogarty, 2006).

In addition to critical thought involved in HOTS, creative thinking needs to be stressed. Here, pupils come up with novel, unique approaches, as in problem solving. Problems need to be identified by students with teacher guidance. Problems generally pertain to vagueness in learner understandings of subject-matter. The problems must have clarity in identification. Information then must be gathered from, a variety of sources such as the internet, reading sources, and subject matter specialists to develop clarifications. Input from students and the teacher, too, assist in securing information for problems identified. Answers involve hypotheses for evaluation. Students need to think of information as being tentative, and not as being final or an absolute. The information secured is the best possible information, developmental appropriate for students. Creative methods are involved in working harmoniously with others in solving problems. Synthesizing ideas is salient in using and evaluation information sources as well as assessing the ideas gleaned. Creative thinking might also stress helping students come up with novel ideas such as in brain storming for an explanation or cause. This activity centres around students generating ideas pertaining to a query. Each response is recorded to avoid duplication of ideas presented. Ridiculing or belittling responses is prohibited. Responses at the end of the session may be grouped into similar categories. Generalizations can then be developed and these must be as rational/accurate as possible (Shridevi, K.V., 2007).

The High School Principal and Leadership in Workshop Development

There are plethora of possibilities in workshops pertaining to reading across the high school curriculum. One procedure is to survey high school teachers to ascertain which problems are faced by students. Might reading of subject-matter be one of these? Different categories should appear on the survey with reading problems being one, among others. Much reading is done by high school students in the different classes being taken. Results from the survey may be used to do a workshop. Questions which the writer has include the following (Ediger, 2007a/b) :

- do students fail to complete assignments due to reading and writing problems?
- are absences from school, in whole or in part, due to a lack of reading skills?
- are students embarrassed/fail to take part in discussions because of not having understood ideas contained in the reading assignment?
- are provisions made in high school to identify and assist those experiencing difficulties in reading?

It is difficult to secure data on the above-named problems. The writer became concerned about reading problems of adults from different observational situations. One being that a few neighbors were somewhat illiterate living near to the writer's rural home, while he was serving as a university professor and supervisor of student teachers in the public schools. One person could merely sign his name to reveal literacy. In adult religious studies groups, participants are asked to read aloud sections of scripture. It must make for feelings of adult insecurity when reading common words aloud, in a very hesitating manner. More of these individuals need assistance to become better readers to meet work place requirements as well as for reading for personal enjoyment.

A second inservice programme might be quite open ended in having teachers intrinsically mention problems faced by high school students in reading. A lively, engaging discussion might well follow. Reading problems may show up not only in poor quality assignments turned in by students, but also in responding late or not at all. Plagiarism may be due to faulty reading and writing traits. The writer believes that the total human being reflects, in part, failures/successes in learning to read and write. Being a good reader may not be praised openly in society, but it is criticized much if failure occurs (Wallace, 2007).

A third inservice education programme may consist of discussing relevant concepts to incorporate in reading across the curriculum. Students possessing adequate background information to benefit from the ensuing reading assignment is important. Thus, the learner must make connections between what he/she knows and and what is to be acquired. Perceiving these relationships helps the student to bridge the gap between the two. Improved comprehension results when the student uses background information possessed to understand new ideas to be read. Advance organizers, selected background information presented to students prior to the ensuing reading activity, is recommended. The new subject matter being read will then sound more familiar to students. Also, new vocabulary must be introduced and understood to attach meaning to subject-matter read. Many times, students fail to read meaningfully due to inadequate vocabulary development. The teacher can print in clear manuscript letters, the new vocabulary terms on the chalkboard, prior to the student reading the new assignment. This will assist students, too, to identify unknown words. As the number of new vocabulary terms introduced per page of content read increases, the complexity of ideas read will increase for the student. Adequate time must be given to clarify the subject matter (Ediger, 2002).

Perceiving purpose helps the student to accept reasons for engagement in the reading experience. The teacher may state a purpose in a few sentences, making certain that students understand these reasons. There are vital reasons for reading academic subject matter. To become a good reader is salient in all walks of life, including its importance in reading materials dealing with technical education, such as reading a manual for car repair services. The writer noticed an automobile mechanic securing a manual for repair work on an older car model. He read the complex content quickly and then proceeded to finish his work on the car engine. Nobody had ever told him that he was a good reader in school! If students perceive purpose in reading, the energy level for learning is there. Then too, rewarding student progress fairly and honestly is salient.

Understanding how ideas are structured is significant for the student. Thus, selected key ideas need to be presented to the learner prior to reading the ensuing subject matter. The key content may be thought of as salient generalizations and main ideas which provide a framework in attaching meaning to subject-matter read. Generalizations/main ideas involve broadly stated subject matter covering content read. Generally, there are two to three main ideas within a chapter of subject matter read. Each is supported by several generalizations. Chapter content may be divided by the author into a certain number of broadly stated main ideas and generalizations. Students need to be introduced to a basal textbook by viewing the chapter titles, the divisions within the chapter, and respective subheadings. Bold print indicates the major divisions and subheadings. With the bold print, students are better able to organize content read. There are a plethora of ideas to read and these need to be properly organized so that a mass number of unrelated sentences do not hinder attaching meaning to subject matter read (Dymock, 2007).

Above all, interest in subject-matter being studied must be emphasized. A variety of challenging learning experiences must be in the offing. The internet, library books, project methods, problem solving experiences, oral reports, cooperative learning activities, inductive and deductive approaches, audio visuals, as well as hands on approaches, among others, should motivate students to increase comprehension in reading related subject matter (Ediger, 2007a/b).

References

Dymock, Susan (2007), "Comprehension Strategy Instruction: Teaching Narrative Text Awareness," *The Reading Teacher*, 61 (2), 168-174.

Ediger, Marlow (2002), "The Supervisor of the School," *Education*, 122 (3), 602-604.

Ediger, Marlow (2006), "Scaffolding in the Reading Curriculum," *Iowa Educational Leadership*, (4), 24-26.

Ediger, Marlow (2007a), "Learning Activities in the Classroom," *College Student Journal*, 41 (4), 967-969.

Ediger, Marlow (2007b), "Teacher Observation to Assess Student Achievement," *Journal of Instructional Psychology*, 34 (3), 137-139.

Ediger, Marlow, and D. Bhaskara Rao (2007), *Reading Curriculum and Instruction*. New Delhi, India: Discovery Publishing House.

Reis, Sally M., and Elizabeth Fogarty, "Savoring Reading, Schoolwide," *Educational Leadership*, 64 (2), 32-36.

Shridevi, K. V. (2007), "Constructivism: A Shift in the Paradigm of Teaching-Learning Process," *Edutracks*, 7 (4), 9-13. Published in India.

Wallace, Christopher (2007), "Vocabulary: The Key to Teaching English Language Learners to Read," *Reading Improvement*, 44 (4), 189-193.

CHAPTER 7

A Constructivist Reading Curriculum

Constructivism is somewhat opposite of a mandated curriculum. It does not emphasize testing to ascertain pupil achievement. Nor is it a teacher determined reading curriculum. A formal reading curriculum with measurably stated objectives would not harmonize with constructivist thinking. Flexibility is a key concept in describing, in part, its basic beliefs about the teaching of reading. Which psychology then best stresses, constructivism?

Teaching and Learning in Reading Instruction

Pupils need to be heavily involved in choosing reading materials. Sequence resides within the pupil, not the teacher nor in textbooks. Thus, sequential library books chosen by the pupil might well make for pupil growth in reading achievement. A variety of genera need to be available to provide for pupils with diverse interests. A pupil may then select which book is of interest to read. Interest is a powerful factor in leaning. Intrinsically, the learner chooses library books for reading. A committee who choose to read the same book might well reveal high levels of comprehension when ideas circulate within the group. Developmentally, each pupil contributes in discussions. When ready, pupils engage in critical and creative thinking, as well as problem solving (Ediger and Rao, 2007a). Processes, too, are salient in that respect for the thinking of others must be in evidence. Abrupt statements, ridicule, and rudeness, as well as hostile statement have no place in the discussion setting.

There are a plethora of uses which may be made of content read. These include :

- creative dramatics within a group or pantomiming for a single individual.
- drawing specific scenes related to subject matter read.
- question the author (QtA) sessions in which all content is subject to questioning.
- reciprocal reading involving purposeful learnings.
- conferences with the teacher to assess comprehension.
- writing poetry involving story content.
- developing parts from a story to be presented in a formal dramatization. Role playing by each child for the part given in the formal dramatization needs to be accurate and meaningful.
- a reader's theater presentation to be given to the entire class and, preferably, visiting classrooms also (Ediger and Rao, 2007b).

Each of the above activities stresses much learner input into the reading curriculum. Teacher leadership is necessary to encourage and stimulate learning. The selection of content and the uses made thereof emphasize pupil responsibility. Pupil and teacher observations are made of learner processes and products. The observations made provide feedback to pupils as positive means for improving the reading curriculum. Pupils largely order their individual learnings (Ediger, 2002).

A rich literature curriculum may also be stressed with read alouds. The teacher reading aloud to children must emphasize literature which captures learner interest. By observing what pupils read in terms of genera and what they talk about, the teacher has a good gauge as to which read alouds might interest children. The teacher must model quality oral reading skills. Proper voice inflection, stress, and pitch assists in securing pupil interest. For young children, it is good to show the related illustrations as the read aloud continues.

Learners should not be passive during the oral reading experience. The teacher needs to pause to raise questions during the read aloud. The questions need to be developmental appropriate and capture learner attention. Questions about the lead character might include, "Have you known people like that?" "What were they interested in?" "What do you think she will do next?" Questions should stress higher levels of cognition as in critical and creative thinking. Inferential thinking, too, is good to emphasize when appropriate. Thus, pupils may be active listeners and respond to questions raised by the teacher as well as those identified by children. Learners are then involved in sequencing their own learnings (Roberts and Billings, 2008).

Read alouds should stimulate interest in literature. Pupils sometimes read the same books which were read aloud. Practice in reading is needed to develop good readers. Pupils who read well tend to continue to do much reading and find it enjoyable at the same time. They need to perceive that content read relates to themselves. Connections also need to be made to others as well as the environment when enjoying literature. Thus, content is related and not to be perceived as isolated bits of information (Keefe, 2007).

Problem-solving is a good way of viewing ideas as being related. Narrative content may be used as well as expository subject matter. An identified problem requires indepth information for a solution. A variety of reference sources need to be used. An hypothesis must be developed followed by its evaluation. Thus, within a social studies unit on the Middle East, the following problem areas may be selected :

- how should the land of Palestine be divided between Arabs and Jews?
- why is the walled city of Jerusalem holy to both Arabs and Jews?
- what importance is the mosque of Abraham in Hebron to opposing sides?
- why are each of the following significant: The Dome of the Rock, the Western Wall, and the Church of the Holy Sepulcher?

Problems need to engage learners and possess purpose. Interest in the problem and its solution makes for effort in learning. Motivation then is high for achieving. Problem solving is quite open ended and pupils learn to accept more of ambiguity in life. Much of life is like this and pupils need to experience the openness of a situation sequentially. Working together, whereby each committee member does his/her fair share of the work, might well be truly stimulating, intellectually, with higher levels of thinking involved. The attitudinal dimension is equally salient. Pupils need to develop wholesome attitudes toward each other, the task at hand, and toward situations which require effort in arriving at solutions to problems. Creative solutions to problems are musts (Reilly, 2007).

Poetry in the Reading Curriculum

In addition to narrative and expository reading, creative reading may be stressed with lessons/units on poetry. To introduce a unit on poetry or integrate it into the ongoing lesson or unit of study, the teacher may plan a quality bulletin board of illustrations showing well known poets. A caption needs to provide readiness for the display. The illustrations must be clear and draw learner attention. A brief biographical sketch pertaining to each may be discussed with children. As much as possible, pupils should be involved in developing the bulletin board. During the introduction, pupils need encouragement to raise questions. These questions might well propel the discussion to provide for increased pupil participation and leadership.

Many pupils enjoy rhyme in poetry. Couplets, triplets, quatrains, and limericks come in this category. After hearing and seeing good models of rhyme in poetry, pupils need to read selected poems. They may desire to make a collection of different kinds of poetry. Favorite poems collected may include those which are based on syllables, such as haiku with its five, seven, five numbers of syllables respectively per line. Five, seven, five, seven, seven syllables per line respectively make for a tanka. Many poems are characterized as free verse with no rhyme nor syllabication needed. These types also interest a plethora of learners.

Pupils need to enjoy poetry. The enjoyment of poetry may be followed by brain storming the meaning of selected poems. Respect for the thinking of contributions in brain storming encourage active participation. Writing poems individually or collectively, and then sharing written verse with others may well motivate interest in poetry. To increase interest in the study of and writing of poetry, the teacher may introduce selected poetic elements to pupils when readiness is in evidence. These poetic elements include :

- alliteration whereby two or more sequential words begin with the same sound.
- onomatopoeia in which words make an echoic sound
- imagery where creative comparisons are made, for example, the sky looks like wandering sheep in the horizon (Ediger, 2007).

Library books containing poetry, along with other genera, should be located at the reading center. Poems may be introduced to pupils by :

- reading aloud in a stimulating manner selected portions of different poems. Thus, pupils, individually, may volunteer to read the rest of an introduced poem.

- suggesting individual projects to be developed based on selected poems.
- monitoring and encouraging work done on these projects.
- encouraging pupil's reading of poetry related to ongoing science, social studies, and mathematics, units of study.

Multicultural poetry/literature should be emphasized to provide for the needs and interests of English Language Learners (ELL). The ELL pupils come from diverse nations and tend to speak a language, in whole or in part, which is different from the local, dominant language. Topics studied need to refer to a variety of genre. They need to stress different cultures. Foods eaten, types of clothing worn, recreational activities, religious beliefs, kinds of homes, means of transportation,among other items, give a culture its identity. Pupils need to understand and appreciate contributions made in society by those of different cultural groups.

Literature circles are one procedure to use which fosters multicultural education. Here, pupils within a small group, discuss the contents of a selected library book. Quality group dynamics must be at the center of literature circle processes. Put downs, name calling, impoliteness, and harassment in their different forms have no roles to play in literature circles. The small group of five to seven have the contents to be discussed well in mind. Literal comprehension now is use as a springboard for moving up the cognitive level. Content then needs to be analyzed for assessment purposes. Evaluation of each facet in the analysis procedure aids in indepth understanding. Following the analyzing, pupils must tie together and synthesize related subject matter. The synthesized subject matter may also be used to solve an identified problem. The worth of the inherent ideas is then appraised in terms of its value in arriving at a solution to a problematic situation.

The teacher's role is to assist pupils in moving forward in thinking within the framework of literature circles. Lecturing and dictating do not harmonize with a constructivist reading curriculum. Rather, pupils are fully engaged in taking leadership roles in assessing ideas presented within a literature circle. Responsibilities rest upon literature circle members. Sequential learnings reside within participants (O'Dell and Jones, 2007).

References

Ediger, Marlow (2002), "The Supervisor of the School," *Education,* 122 (3),602-604.

Ediger, Marlow (2007), "Reading and Writing Poetry," *South Dakota Reading Council Journal*, 11 (1), 8-10.

Ediger, Marlow, and D. Bhaskara Rao (2007a), *Reading Curriculum and Instruction*. New Delhi, India: Discovery Publishing House.

Ediger, Marlow, and D. Bhaskara Rao (2007b), *English Education*. New Delhi, India: Discovery Publishing House.

Keefe, James W. (2007), "What is Personalization?" *Phi Delta Kappa,* 89 (3), 217-223.

O'Dell, Chantelle, and Joanna Jones (2007)," The Circle of Literature Circles: Critical Thinking Communities," *South Dakota Reading Council Journal*, 11 (1), 11-19.

Reilly, Mary Ann (2007), "Choice of Action; Using Data to Make Instructional Decisions in Kindergarten," 60 (8), 770- 776.

Roberts, Terry, and Laura Billings (2008), "Thinking is Literacy, Literacy Thinking," *Educational Leadership,* 65 (5), 32-37.

CHAPTER 8

School Principal as a Reading Supervisor

The role of the principal has changed from being a manager of a school to a leader in curriculum improvement. With mandated testing, it behooves the school principal to assist in improving the curriculum. Increased accountability of teachers for pupil achievement is in the offing. Reading as a curriculum area is basic to success in the different academic disciplines taught in school. This manuscript will pertain to the principal working with teachers to strengthen the reading programme.

The Principal and the Reading Curriculum

How might the school principal assist teachers to improve reading instruction? Certainly, he/she needs to be well versed in what makes for quality teaching and learning situations in reading. Word recognition causes problems for pupils. Helping pupils to use context clues is a major way of identifying unknown words. If a pupil is unable to recognize a word, he/she may use a word that fits in meaningfully. Reading the surrounding words/sentences will further ascertain if a pupil has identified the unknown word correctly. Then too, if a pupil can sound out the initial consonant of the unknown word, the chances are the word which makes sense within the sentence will be correct (Ediger and Rao, 2007).

There are critics who advocate more phonics be taught. This may be a good recommendation if the graphemes (letters) harmonize with the related phonemes. The are sounds and symbols which harmonize as in the following words - run, sun, fun. There are, however, words which rhyme with the preceding, but are spelled differently - done, none - as well as words spelled the same for the latter set, except for the initial consonant, but are pronounced differently - bone, lone, tone. Phonics is valuable in teaching up to a point when sound/ symbol relationships do not exist. There can be consistency even in parts of a word such as phone. The "n" sound is the only consistently spelled grapheme. It does, however, follow the pattern of consonanWowel/consonant/silent "e" patterns making for a long vowel sound of "o."

Learning words through the sight method will need to be used when other procedures do not work. Sight word may be printed on a three by four inch cards; pupifs might then practices identifying each as it is being viewed (Ediger, 2007)

For primary grade pupils, using picture clues to identify an unknown word will heip, in many cases, to identify unknown words. Thus, if a pupil cannot recognize a word, the picture in the page of the textbook will give away its pronunciation. Generally, pictures in books are many and large for young children. Hopefully a picture will provide the clue for the child in determining an unknown word (Gunning, 2000).

The school principal needs to provide leadership in helping teachers also teach struggling readers. Struggling readers need teacher assistance to determine where each pupils is presently in reading achievement. This may be done by having teachers mark one hundred running words in the basal text being used. The struggling reader may then read aloud to the teacher that marked portion. He/she has not heard the selection read nor practiced it in silent reading. Thus, the struggling reader may reveal his/her reading level presently. If the pupil reads 95 per cent or more of the running words correctly, as well as answering four out of four comprehension questions correctly, the text is on the pupil's recreational reading level. This is the level of words read correctly for enjoyment purposes from a library book. Reading correctly 85 to 94 per cent of the running words correctly represents the instructional level, providing that three out of four questions are answered correctly covering the contents read. Going below that level in word recognition and comprehension, the pupil tends to read on the frustration level. From the instructional level of the text being the starting point, the teacher may develop objectives, learning activities, and evaluation procedures. The instructional level provides opportunities for the struggling reader to be successful with quality sequence and good teaching (Devine, 1986).

For all levels of pupil reading progress, the principal needs to help teachers with recreational reading. Here, pupils choose their very own library books individually and silently read to the self. Generally, pupils choose library books to read which are interesting and on the appropriate reading level. Interest is a powerful factor in learning and propels the learner to read sequentially more complex levels of reading materials. The teacher observes if pupils individually are fully engaged in reading. Conferences may be held with individual pupils to check oral reading proficiency as well as comprehension of content. Notes of the conference may be recorded and progress noticed by the teacher in future reading conferences (Ediger, 2002).

Higher Order Thinking Skills

It is salient for pupils to realize higher order thinking skills in reading. The principal may provide leadership in guiding teachers to assist pupils in diverse kinds of thinking while reading. Literal interpretation is necessary, but pupils need to learn to think at a more complex level. The recall level then involves literal comprehension. But to truly comprehend well, the pupil must read analytically. Here, the learner separates facts from opinions, accurate from inaccurate statements, as well as fantasy from reality. When reading editorials in newspapers, the pupil needs to think critically pertaining to opinions read. Also, it is always good to attempt to check the accuracy of ideas read. Synthesizing, too, is salient in that once inaccuracies, for example, have been taken out, then the reader must put together what is accurate in a complete thought.

Reading creatively also stresses higher order thinking in that the pupil comes up with unique ideas in interpreting news happenings and events. Creative thinking has made for progress in society in that someone needs to think of better processes, products, and ways of doing things. It emphasizes what is unique and original.

Scaffolding is an important concept to use in reading instruction. Thus, if achieving an objective appears to be too complex, the teacher may assist the learner to bridge the gap between the known and the unknown. This involves sequencing learnings until the objective has been attained by the pupil. In the past, the thinking was that if a pupil cannot attain an objective, no more effort need be put forth. With scaffolding, however, there are good chances of bridging the gap between the known and the unknown (Yopp and Yopp, 2007).

Inservice Education

The school principal must take the lead in promoting inservice education programs to improve instruction. Phonics versus whole language approaches in reading very often take center stage in this debate. The former have strong backers in having teachers teach sound/symbol relationships in assisting pupils to read. They believe that if pupils learn to decode effectively, reading progress will be shown by learners. Somewhat toward the other end of the continuum, whole language advocates unveil their approaches in teaching reading. There are several procedures which might be emphasized here :

- the big book approach stresses using a large book for all pupils in small groups of five or six, approximately, be able to see the contents clearly. The teachers comments on the illustrations and encourages input from learners in the discussion. This provides background information to pupils as well as assists pupils to posses the necessary facts and concepts to understand the ensuing content. The teacher then reads aloud the content, pointing to each word being read, as pupils follow along in the big book. Next, pupils read aloud with the teacher as the latter again points to each word encountered. With the third reading, the same procedure is followed as in the previous step of reading aloud. The fourth time, pupils, only, read aloud, the content with the teacher observing the ongoing experience. This activity may be repeated as often as needed or desired. Here, pupils are reading content without hindrance/embarrassment of not being able to recognize individual words or phrases, A basic sight word vocabulary for reading is then being developed by pupils. If desired, phonics may be stressed in the following examples in the selection just read aloud :

    1. who can find a word which begins like "dog?"
    2. who can find a word which ends like "cat?"
    3. who can find a word which rhymes with "man?"

- a second inservice education activity might well emphasize individualized reading. Here, the teacher introduces a few library books to pupils in class. The library books need to be appealing, interesting and meet pupil needs. Learners may then select books to read sequentially. At intervals, a conference needs to be held. The teacher checks oral reading progress of the pupil, as well as comprehension through related questions discussed. Conference information needs to be filed for future reference and comparison.

Individualized reading stresses that pupils are in the best position to choose reading materials based on personal interests and reading level possessed. This approach can be used solely or with other approaches in reading instruction such as the use of basai readers.

Additional inservice education procedures include the following :

- surveying teachers to ascertain which problems they face in reading. Items listed might well provide the basis for an inservice program.
- demonstration teaching of "Questioning the Author" (QtA), followed by an indepth discussion.
- panel presentation on implementing "Reciprocal Reading," followed by questions from inservice education participants (Biddle and Sana 2006).

Teachers need to try, in their respective classrooms, different approaches elaborated upon from inservice education sessions. Obtaining feedback to report to inservice education participants is truly worthwhile.

References

Biddle, Bruce J., and Lawrence J. Saha, "How Principals Use Research," *Educational Leadership*, 63 (6), 72-78.

Devine, T. G. (1986), *Teaching Reading Comprehension*. Boston: Allyn and Bacon, Inc.

Ediger, Marlow (2002), "The Supervisor of the School," *Education*, 122 (3), 602-604.

Ediger, Marlow (2007), "The Substitute Teacher in Reading Instruction," *The Sub-Journal*, 8 (2), 67-73.

Ediger, Marlow, and D. Bhaskara Rao (2007), *Reading Curriculum and Instruction*. New Delhi, India: Discovery Publishing House.

Gunning, Thomas (2000), *Creating Literacy Instruction for All children*. Needham Heights, Massachusetts; Allyn and Bacon, Inc.

Yopp, Helen Ruth, and Hollie K. Yopp (2007), "Ten Important Words Plus: A Strategy for Building Word Knowledge," *The Reading Teacher*, 61 (2), 157-160.

CHAPTER 9

Strategies in Reading Instruction

The reading instructor needs to use a variety of strategies to encourage student reading achievement. Strategies used must meet learner needs. Meeting diagnosed needs assists the teacher in providing adequately for each student in the classroom. The needs of each student may differ from that of others; however, there will be some overlapping. Students need to achieve as optimally as possible. It is salient then for the reading teacher to possess excellent knowledge and skills in how to assist students to attain relevant objectives in the curriculum.

Strategies of Teaching and Learning

Strategy instruction has received much emphasis in professional literature. Teachers should assist students to use different strategies in ongoing learning activities in assisting learners to attain more optimally (Ediger, 2006). This is especially true for students who experience difficulty in learning such as in reading and writing. Difficulties in learning may be ameliorated with effective instruction. Early teaching to use each strategy well is needed. Systematic teaching also needs to be in evidence. Explicit teaching may not be adequate to help certain pupils learn to use these tools effectively. Students may use specific strategies during explicit teaching, but fail to use them during independent study time. They also need guidance to apply each strategy. Tools of the trade may be taught through the use of *physical objects* such as :

- looking for the word on the word wall.
- finding a word which will assist in spelling and in word identification such as could-should.
- locating the word in a dictionary.
- noticing if the word is in print in the classroom environment, in addition to the word wall.

Tools of the *mind* include the following used strategies :

- saying the word slowly and listening for sounds heard.
- thinking of different spelling patterns that can spell the sound one hears, out vs down.
- say the word slowly and listen for parts that are known in spelling, and in candy.
- think about the word and notice if it can be seen mentally.
- think of a word which rhymes that one is attempting to spell (Williams and Lundstrom, 2007).

The tools of the trade may be used in both reading and writing. For example, an unknown word may be recognized by looking on the word wall in the classroom for a similarly spelled word. Each student needs to be cognizant of monitoring his/her own achievement in reading. The monitoring must be ongoing as the leaner evaluates continuously if subject matter read is understood. Retelling what has been read is one approach to the monitoring one's own progress. Merely reading words without comprehension does not suffice in monitoring the self in an ongoing reading activity (Ediger, 2007).

Monitoring vocabulary growth and development aids the student to ascertain which words are meaningful or lack understanding. Those vocabulary terms not understood become objectives to achieve. With the use of context clues or dividing an unknown word into syllables helps the learner to read meaningfully. Skipping over unidentified words may add to increased reading difficulties later on. Growth and development needs to be sequential and continuous. Thus, the student in monitoring the self-notices if subject matter and vocabulary terms are understood. Teaching and learning strategies must emphasize students monitoring their very own individual achievement and progress (Reis and Fogarty, 2006).

Second, self-efficacy needs to be achieved by learners. Here, the student develops confidence in the self through sequential progress experienced in reading. Success in learning is sequential and continuous, making for an increasingly positive self concept. Feelings of being able to successfully read/comprehend well and do things to achieve relevant goals are inherent in feelings of self-efficacy. How is this to be done?

- sequence learnings in reading so that the student perceives progress, not failure.
- adjust the reading curriculum to the present achievement level of the learner and then optimize successful progress.
- assist the student to experience subsequent progress.
- provide adequate feedback of student progress so the latter receives knowledge of results in order to benefit from the ensuing activities.
- have the learner experience appropriate readiness activities in reading to benefit fully from the ensuing experiences.
- help the student to relate previous learnings to the new subject-matter to be acquired (Ediger and Rao (2007).

Success in learning helps the student to become more confident in his/her abilities. Growth in achievement assists the student in developing a more adequate self concept. He/she leans more upon the self to solve problems and answer questions. The student then has had numerous opportunities to have esteem needs met. Recognition for progress made in order to benefit fully from the ensuing activities, should promote feelings of confidence. Feeling confident with a good self image makes for positive attitudes in being successful in the new and novel tasks which abound (Noyagam, 2006).

Third, metacognition strategies used assist the learner to review, rehearse, evaluate and come up with a new synthesis of ideas. In having read subject-matter, the student may think about what was acquired in terms of facts, concepts, and generalizations. Clarity of ideas might have been missing and the learner notices what needs additional clarification. Problems may be identified through metacognition. An hypothesis may be developed pertaining to the identified problem, resulting in information sought from a variety of reference sources. The hypothesis is then tested.

Factors involved in metacognitive thinking include the following :

- analyzing one's own comprehension from reading, discussions, and group work.
- using the instructional component according to one's analyzed needs.
- determining background information necessary for acquisition of ensuing ideas.
- selecting and utilizing a specific strategy for learning.
- clarifying each strategy.
- monitoring the effectiveness of strategy used.
- evaluating strategies used.
- assessing subject-matter achieved (Savithiri, 2006).

For the teacher of reading, the above metacognitive strategy involves helping the learner to use critical thinking to appraise his/her ideas gained from the ongoing activity. Then the student needs assistance to choose a method of procedure such as reading to secure an answer to a question. The learner must retrieve background information in order to benefit from the ensuing reading activity. The learner needs to possess clarity on the strategy to be used in securing answers to questions or problems. The student should monitor his own effectiveness in the strategy used. Reading involves comprehending ideas and evaluating secured subject-matter.

Metacognition may also be stressed in transcript analysis. Here, for example, the reading teacher tapes a segment of student discussion pertaining to subject matter read. He/she asks questions pertaining to content discussed in the tape. The questions extend thinking. Thus, answers to questions provided by learners presently become more indepth inclined. Students think about thinking in that the answers to questions given on the tape form a basis for elaboration. They review what was said on the tape and then bring in additional and new ideas. The relationship between the old and then new make for a synthesis (Savithiri, 2006).

Fourth, a student centred reading curriculum may be emphasized. Here, goals of instruction stress input from learners in the classroom. For example, pupils may present ideas for subject-matter to be read in beginning reading instruction. Objects on an interest center may provide for encoding while pupils watch the process of linking the objects (the concrete situation) with the abstract (words recorded). Pupils present the ideas from observations made of these objects. The teacher then types the commands using the word processor, resulting in words seen on a screen. Pupils might then see talk recorded. They practice reading the ideas as the teacher points to each word in the read aloud. The read aloud may be stressed as often as desired. Many times, pupils like to hear the same content read aloud more than once. It should, however, be read aloud frequently enough as pupils observe each word being read in order to develop a basic sight vocabulary. This is a learner centered reading program in that :

- pupils present the content for encoding which stresses familiarity of subject matter read.
- pupils sequence their very own ideas to be read as they are being presented from objects viewed on the interest centre.
- pupils practice reading aloud their own thinking pertaining to observations made.
- pupils rehearse the read aloud until abstract words are recognized which become a part of their own reading progress (San Antonio, 74-79).

Reading programmes on any age/grade level need to emphasize questions to discuss which come from learners. These questions tend to be of interest to students. Elementary school reading programmes which stress learner input into selecting and sequencing achievement in addition to the above asterisked item include individualized reading, sustained silent reading, the accelerated reader, and the Big Book approach, among others. Teachers of reading need to select those programs which involve considerable learner choice in terms of objectives, learning activities, and appraisal procedures (Keefe, 2007).

CONCLUSION

Students need to experience strategies of instruction which engage, meet needs, optimize achievement, and promote perceived purpose. Reading programs and strategies of instruction must provide for individual differences (Clarke and Holwadel, 2007).

References

Clarke, Lane W., and Jennifer Holwadel (2007), "Help! What is Wrong With These Literature Circles and How Can We Fix Them?" *The Reading Teacher*, 61 (1), 20-31.

Ediger, Marlow (2006), "Administration of Schools," *College Student Journal*, 40 (4), 846-851.

Ediger, Marlow (2007), "Teacher Observation to Evaluate Achievement," *Journal of Instructional Psychology*, 34 (3), 137-139.

Ediger, Marlow, and D. Bhaskara Rao (2007), *Reading Curriculum and Instruction.* New Delhi, India: Discovery Publishing House.

Keefe, James W. (2007), "What is Personalization?" *Phi Delta Kappan*, November issue, 217-223.

Noyagam, Soosai, (2006), Constraints and Their Impact on the Academic Achievement of the Santal Tribal 12th STD Students in Jharkhand State, PhD thesis evaluated by the writer for St. Xavier's College of Education, Palayamkottai, India.

Reis, Sally M., and Elizabeth Fogarty (2006), "Savoring Reading, Schoolwide," *Educational Leadership*, 64 (2), 32-36.

San Antonio, Donna Marie (2006), "Understanding Student Strengths and Weaknesses," *Educational Leadership*, 65 (7), 74-79.

Williams, Cheri, and Ruth P. Lundstrom (2007), "Strategy Instruction During Word Study and Interactive Writing," *The Reading Teacher,* 61 (3), 204-211.

Savithiri, V. (2006), Impact of Metacognitive Strategies in Enhancing Perceptual skills Among High School Students on Learning Geometry. Ph D thesis evaluated by the writer for Alagappa University, Karaikudi, India.

CHAPTER 10

Data-based Instruction in Reading

Data based instruction has received much attention in educational literature. It relates well to measurement driven teaching and learning. Data may come from several sources including mandated tests, district wide testing, formative and summative evaluations, as well as teacher written tests.

Objective information is intended for use in data based strategy of teaching and learning. Information secured from pupil test results deemed objective measurements provide teachers needed information in assisting pupils to achieve well.

Data-based Reading Instruction

Data from test results provide objectives for instruction. Machine scoring is generally used; however in the case of teacher written tests, hand scoring may be more convenient. From computer printouts, the teacher has knowledge of what pupils missed and what is left to learn. Learning activities, aligned with these objectives, help learners to achieve the precise objectives. Objectives must be stated with precision so that little/no leeway exists for their interpretation. It must be measurable if the objectives have/have not been achieved after instruction. Individual differences need to be provided for since achievement levels from test results will vary (Ediger, 2009).

With mandated testing in the different states, many are using standardized tests, already published, or have been designed for a state to harmonize with stated, specific objectives of instruction. The standardized tests generally have been pilot tested in a representative sampling of students. Standardized means that those taking the test receive the same test items for their age or grade level, the directions given are the same, as are the time limits for test taking. The tests are valid if they measure what is purported to be evaluated, such as a test measuring pupil achievement in word recognition, measure something different such as grammar, syntax, and semantics. If the standardized test is based on knowledge of grammar, then this is what needs to be tested in order to be valid.

Equally salient as compared to validity is the concept of reliability. Thus, a test needs to measure consistently with either test/retest, split half, and/or alternate forms reliability. The Manual accompanying the standardized test provides information on validity and how it was ascertained as well as reliability data. Pupil test results are then compared from the given standardized test to pilot tested information contained in the Manual. Student test results will be given in percenttles, generally, but also might include grade equivalent, age equivalent, and stanine scores. Thus, a student may be on the forty fifth percentile, based on others who had taken the same test in the pilot studies representing the norms contained in the Manual (Ediger, 2008a).

There are standardized tests in reading which cover a plethora of objectives such as reading comprehension in general, critical reading, problem solving, creative reading, phonics skills, and word recognition, among others. Useful information about pupils may be attained if these tests possess high validity as well as reliability. Standardized test then provide information in data driven decision-making.

Standardized tests are given once in a school year and thus do not provide data on pupil achievement during each day of the school year. Teacher written tests then also become salient. Multiple choice tests written by classroom teachers need to follow quality standards of writing test items and these include the following :

- each of the four distractors must be plausible. An unreasonable distractor may be immediately eliminated by the pupil. Thus, fewer than four distractors provide more opportunities for guessing the correct response of a multiple choice test item.
- the four distractors need to be of similar length so as not to provide clues as to which is correct.
- each distractor must be grammatically correct with the stem. This also minimizes chances for guessing the correct response. Selected teacher written test items may have no stem, e.g. which of the following words is spelled incorrectly :

  (*a*) manager (*b*) sincerely (*c*) lumber (*d*) ample.
- face validity needs to be used in that the teacher writes the test items which cover what has been taught.
- the test must be written on the developmental level of learners (Ediger, 2008b).

True/false teacher written tests have merit if quality test writing is involved and pupils need to correct the part of a test item, if it is incorrect. Securing the correct answer is a 50 per cent possibility unless the pupil must correct the incorrect part of a test item. Notice the following incorrectly written true/false test item :

> The following words represent alliteration—pizza, pie, put, sell. The word "sell" is incorrect since it does not begin with the same sound as the others.

Matching tests may be beneficial to measure pupil knowledge of vital facts. There needs to be more items in one column as compared to the other so that the process of elimination is minimized. Column A is then matched with items in column B. Lengthy sentences should not be written for each column since it becomes difficult to keep all the information in mind for matching purposes. Thus in column A, important concepts may be written such as synonyms; antonyms; acronyms; metaphors; hyperbole, slang; idioms; oxymoron; personification; homophones. Column B contains brief definitions for matching with the correct concept in column A (Baumann *et al.* 2007).

Each kind of teacher written test should provide feedback to both teachers and pupils as to what needs more emphasis in teaching and learning situations. Test data should inform which objectives need more stress in the curriculum.

Essay tests might well provide much information on pupil progress in an ongoing lesson/unit of study. These tests must have questions which are not factual, nor do they require a chapter in their writing. Pupil written responses may be assessed using a quality rubric to insure more objective grading. Thus, the following need appraisal :

- analysis, synthesis, and evaluation in the written product, depending upon which are valid for testing
- use of complete sentences
- clarity of ideas expressed
- correct grammar and spelling of words.

The following are examples of essay test items :

- Take a character from any story studied and change him/her into a different being which fits into that story setting.
- Why do you think the actual character in a different story chose his/her future as was done?
- Write a summary of the setting of different stories studied in the just completed unit of study (See Atmasi, 2003).

In writing any kind of test item age/grade, and ability levels of learners must be taken into thorough consideration. The use of precise objectives works well with data driven decision-making since clarity of information is desired from pupils as a result of the latter experiencing appropriate learning activities. The learning activities must be aligned with the stated objectives. This makes it possible to secured data from assessment results, which in turn, drives instruction (Pettyjohn and Sacco, 2007).

Contrasting Data Driven Decision with Constructivism

Constructivism uses other procedures of in teaching to secure information on pupil progress than testing. With constructivism, the following, among others, are salient :

- teacher observation of pupils in every day lessons when the latter learn by discovery. Testing is minimized.
- pupil self-evaluation with teacher guidance.
- the teacher assists pupils in specific learning opportunities to reflect upon difficulties and come up with a satisfactory answer.
- pupil interests, questions, and feelings become a part of ongoing units of study.
- learning is social and small group endeavors are important in discussing content (See Vygotsky, 1978).

References

Almasi, J. (2003), *Teaching Specific Processes in Reading.* New York: Guilford.

Baumann, James F. et.al. (2007), "Bumping into Spicy, Testy Words That Catch Your Tongue. A Formative Experiment in Vocabulary Instruction," *The Reading Teacher*, 61 (2), 108-122.

Ediger, Marlow (2008), Leadership in the School Setting," *Education*, 129 (1), 17-20.

Ediger, Marlow (2008b), "The American High School," College Student Journal, 42(3), 814-817.

Ediger, Marlow (2009), "For an Effective Reading Program," *Reading Improvement,"* 46(3), 119-122.

Pettyjohn, Terry F, and Matthew F. Sacco (2007), "Multiple-Choice Exam Questions Order Influence on Student Performance, Completion Time, and Performance," *Journal of Instructional Psychology,* 34 (3), 142-149.

Vygotsky, L. S. (1978), Mind in Society : *The Development of Higher Psychological Processes.* Cambridge, MA : Harvard University Press.

CHAPTER 11

Student and Language Arts

There are selected learnings in the language arts which provide structure in the English language. These concepts and generalizations provide students with strategies for study and analysis. A richer reading, writing, listening, and speaking vocabulary might then emerge. Sequential learnings are necessary here in order to make for continuous student progress. Which needed objectives are necessary for learner achievement?

Poetry and the Language Arts

There are ingredients in poetry that might well assist pupils in understanding creative elements. Rhyme is a factor in assisting pupils to appreciate different types of poems. Poems which rhyme include couplets (two lines with ending words rhyming), triplets (three lines of rhyme), quatrains (four lines of rhyme), and limericks (lines one, two, and five, as well as lines three and four rhyme :

- Poems may also contain a certain number of syllables per line as in haiku with three lines having five, seven, five, syllables respectively per line. Add two more lines with seven syllables per line making for a tanka.

- Free verse contains no rhyme or syllabication, necessarily, and the length per line is open ended (Ediger, 2007).

The teacher needs to read different types of poetry aloud to students. The read aloud needs to emphasize appropriate stress, pitch, and intonation to capture learner attention. Students need to see these kinds of poems in print. Enjoyment of poetry is a major objective of instruction. Thus, students may wish to make a collection of diverse forms of poetry, containing different topics. These are poems which are of interest and enlist learner enthusiasm.

Additional elements which poets include in writing poems include the following :

- *alliteration*. Two or more successive words containing the same initial sound as in "slurping sweet soup."
- *onomatopoeia*. Echoic sounding words used to describe such as "bang," "splash," and "ouch."
- *imagery*. Creative comparisons are made such as in "The boy ran like a deer." The underlined tells in a novel way how the boy ran (Labbo, 2004).

In teaching entire units on poetry or in integrating it with social studies, science, or mathematics units of study, the teacher needs to plan lessons which engage and secure student interests. Student purposes, too, are salient. Thus, different genre make for unique selections of poems including holiday, animals, historical, circus, seasons, multi-cultural, and adventure poetry. A variety of magazines and poetry books should be available for student reading as well as models for writing poetry (Arbuthnot, 1959; Wood, 2006).

Memorization of poems should be left up to the student and not required. Many students perceive little purpose in the memorization process. The writer, when in the seventh and eighth grades along with classmates, was required to memorize selected poems. This was a pleasurable experience and still is enriching when rehearsing parts of classical poems today. These poems include :

- "My Shadow" by Robert Louis Stevenson
- "The Vision of Sir Launfel" by James Russell Lowell
- The well known verse, "Over the river and to the woods, to grandmothers house we go....

Memorizing of poetry appears to be a learning style. One of my university colleagues stated that he was not proficient at memorizing but did like to read poetry. This appears to be the case for many adults, spoken to, that some liked to memorize poetry and others did not. Memorizing poems, then, should be voluntary, but might well be encouraged.

Learning Activities

The teacher needs to have a repertoire of methods in teaching poetry. Each student must become engaged in learning, be it within a large or small group as well as individually.

Literature circles provide a social setting in analyzing and synthesizing content. Four to five members in the circle must adhere to rules in working together harmoniously. A major rule, here, is to respect each other's ideas. Then too, ideas need to circulate within the group with each person participating and no one dominating the discussion. Participants have had ample opportunities to read the poems, prior to their being discussed. Readiness is an important factor for participating. Students individually need to be highly responsible for active involvement in the literature circle. Self evaluation, in terms of criteria, should follow each literature circle session. Teacher observation must also be used to appraise achievement of students.

With individualized reading of poetry, the student may have a conference with the teacher on a one on one basis. Several poems read by the student may be discussed. The teacher needs to notice criteria such as comprehension, enjoyment, and enthusiasm in discussing each poem read. The teacher should record items to make comparisons with future conferences.

An art project such as mural development may be developed collectively. Contents in the mural need to illustrate important concepts and/or generalizations. A theme might well be incorporated such as the central idea of the poem(s) illustrated. The theme, for example, may stress "Animals in Poetry." Rich scenes, colours, and creative ideas need to be inherent in the mural.

Additional experiences for students involving poetry include the following :

- reading other poems by the same author or dealing with a similar genre
- choosing poetry to read during time devoted to sustained silent reading (SSR)
- dramatizing a poem for classmates to view
- doing a reader's theater using selected poems
- engaging in reciprocal reading involving poetry.

Metacognition in Reading Poetry

Metacognition involves thinking about thinking. Thus, a student may be taught to monitor comprehension in his/her own reading of poetry. A learner then thinks, involving the self, which ideas have been understood and what needs further clarification. The reflection is salient in that indepth comprehension of ideas and concepts in poetry is assisted through reflection.

In writing of poetry, the student reflects upon what a model limerick is in terms of patterns of rhyme and involved rhythm. He/she may then write a creative limerick. The learner leans upon the self in coming up with creative ideas (Boulware-Gooden *et al.*, 2007).

IN CONCLUSION

It is important to inform parents of many educational endeavors. They might well be a source of assistance in motivating their offspring. Motivation in student's writing poetry is salient. In parent/teacher conferences and in portfolios, the teacher and the learner may show parents what has been accomplished in poetry writing. Creativity is needed in poetry writing as well as in decision making in life (Ediger, 2008).

REFERENCES

Arbuthnot, M. H. (1959), *Time for Poetry*. Chicago, Illinois : Scott, Foresman and Company.

Boulware-Gooden, Regina, *et al.* (2007), "Instruction of Metacognitive Strategies Enhances Reading Comprehension and Vocabulary Achievement of Third-Grade Students," The Reading Teacher, 61 (1), 70-78.

Ediger, Marlow (2007), "Reading and Writing Poetry, South Dakota," *Reading Journal*, 11 (1), 8-10.

Ediger, Marlow (2008), "Psychology of Parental Involvement in Reading," *Reading Improvement*, 45 (1), 46-52.

Labbo, L. D. (2004), "Poetry on the Screen," *The Reading Teacher*, 58 (3), 308-311.

Wood, J. R. (2006), *Living voices, Multi-cultural Poetry in the Middle School Classroom*. Urbana, Illinois: National Council Teachers of English.

CHAPTER 12

Vocabulary Development in Language Arts

Teaching vocabulary development has changed much since the writer attended the public schools from 1934-1946. When attending public schools, the teacher would generally say, "If you don't know the meaning of a word, look it up in the dictionary." A major problem here is that the reader of subject matter loses the trend of sequential thought when looking up the meaning of unknown words being read.

There are more meaningful procedures in finding word meanings when being engaged in reading. The content read needs to follow a certain order and finding the meaning of unknown words violates, in securing these sequential ideas.

Vocabulary Development and the Learner

A reputable dictionary may be one way to extract meanings for words. When listening to a newscast or conversation, the listener might well look up needed meanings at a later convenient time. In this way, the ordered ideas gleaned from listening may be secured in depth. Meaningful experiences are always necessary and are at the heart of learning.

While reading subject-matter, the reader must focus on content read and not have disruptions to look up word meanings. Words which are puzzling may be written down and looked up for meaning, in a dictionary after the act of reading has been completed. During the reading act, the pupil may use context clues to establish meaning for unknown words. Thus, if an unknown word is met, the pupil may continue with decoding and determine the identity of the word or its meaning through context clues. By reading the surrounding words or within the paragraph, the reader generally ascertains the meaning of what was previously unknown. A peer, para-professional, or the teacher may assist in filling in the unknown. Assistance should be available as soon as possible to help with what is not understood. For pupils with severe reading difficulties, learners may listen to a recording of the ideas while following the printed script in the book being used (Ediger and Rao, 2007).

Dyads may be used to helping classmates in reading subject-matter. Thus, twc pupils may study together when reading, be it expository, narrative, or creative writings such as poetry. Additional ways of pupils assisting each other is through a literature circle. Here, three to five pupils may help each other to do meaningful reading. The members in the literature circle may guide each other in ways beyond securing word meanings of words or word recognition, such as in reading at higher cognitive levels, including :

- *critical reading*—separating facts from opinions, fantasy from reality, and accurate from inaccurate statements.
- *creative thinking*—coming up with unique, novel ideas.
- *evaluating ideas read* to ascertain their worth as in problem solving (Ediger, 2007).

When engaged in individualized reading, for example, pupils may find it interesting to look for prefixes which mean "not" when reading a library book of their very own choosing. These may be recorded in a notebook and include such "not" prefixes as "non", "un", "im," "in", and "dis". A suffix hunt might well add to the fascination such as "er" endings meaning "one who" as in singer, dancer, swimmer, and jumper These are common prefixes and suffixes which might well assist pupils in vocabulary development.

Brain-storming for synonyms also provides rich experiences for pupils. When ready, pupils may brainstorm for synonyms including the following: small, wealthy, house. Equally interesting will be brain-storming for antonyms: door, sour, beautiful.

Looking for and suggesting phonetic elements provide further opportunities for vocabulary growth and development. Thus, pupils in the classroom or committee setting may give words with alliteration such as dug, ditch, dog. These words begin with the same initial sound. Or, experimenting with echoic sounding words (onomatopoeia) may motivate learners in searching for words which tend to make their own individual sounds such as "bang," "splash," "wow!" Both alliteration and onomatopoeia should be used in written work, when applicable (Baumann, *et al.* 2007). The writer when supervising university student teachers in the public schools observed a lesson in which pupils used imagery in discussing poetic elements. The following, as examples, were discussed :

- the night was like a candle burning bright. The underlined words represent a comparison between "night" and "like a candle burning bright."
- the boy ran *like a speeding car.*
- the cat slept on the carpet *as if she would never wake up.*

Use of imagery stresses figurative use of language, not literal interpretation. Imagery is used in written work to make for unique interpretations to listeners and readers when literal statements may not do justice to what is being stated. Then, too, figurative language adds variety to content and ideas expressed. The following are interesting :

- Lets stop beating a dead horse.
- Lets step up to the plate and show who we are.
- Have a good one.
- That is the missing part of the equation.

There are two kinds of imagery. Similes use the words "like", and "as" to make creative comparisons, e.g. He ran *like a scared rabbit.* Metaphors omit the words "like" and "as" to make novel comparisons, e.g. The boy made *explosive thundering* sounds.

Homonym hunts may be quite engaging for learners. One student/cooperating teacher in the public schools observed by the writer challenged learners to look up and record homonyms. Different reference books, including the dictionary, were used. Located homonyms included the following: there/there; here/hear; bear/bare; pain/pane. A generalization was developed in that these words are pronounced the same, but individual meanings depend upon their use in a sentence. Additional word classes to be studied include heteronyms, words spelled alike but pronounced differently. In context, the reader may read, "*Separate* the red discs from the blue." In comparison, a sentence may read "They drove in separate cars." The two underlined words are pronounced differently but have the same spelling.

Grammar is considered a dull area of study by many. However, it can be interesting when used as vocabulary study. There are a plethora of approaches which may be used here. The teacher needs to choose sentences which present possibilities for vocabulary growth. Thus in studying simple sentences, a word needs to be omitted such as the subject: The ran a long distance. For the blank space, many words may be put in its place. The names of objects, persons, and animals, among others, may be placed in the blank. Each word should be recorded for all pupils to see so that duplications are not presented. At another time, the predicated of the sentence may be left out, as in, "The car—on the road". Respect for the thinking of others is important. Rudeness has no place in the school setting. The sky is the limit in terms of words to be put into a blank space. In spare time, pupils individually or in small groups, may put in place an adjective or adverb to replace a blank. Rich experiences are needed to challenge the thinking and creativity of learners. Then too, related increasingly more complex learnings may accrue in ensuing lessons, in addition to toying with subjects, predicates, adjectives, and adverbs :

- five basic sentence patterns. Nouns/pronouns as well as adjectives and adverbs might be brainstormed to replace a blank in each sentence pattern.
- sentence types including simple, compound, complex, and compound/complex. Thus, for example, possible dependent clauses may be added to a simple sentence resulting in a complex sentence.
- different adjective and adverb prepositional phrases proposed as modifiers in sentences.
- diverse dependent clauses added which modify nouns and verbs, as well as noun clauses used as the subject of the sentence (Ediger, 2007).

Word Walls in the Classroom

Word walls have become popular in teaching word recognition and identification. Vocabulary development also must be stressed within the word wall concept. Pupils need to be challenged to bring new vocabulary terms to the attention of classmates. These words may be gleaned from diverse kinds of reading materials used in independent reading in the school/home setting. Each word needs to be pronounced clearly by the teacher when it is printed on the word wall for all to see. The new words assist pupils in vocabulary development and each word must be defined or used contextually within a sentence. Review of these words is necessary to aid in retention. Pupils may see the list extending on the word wall. Encouragement in using the words in oral and written communication is salient (Hawkins, 2006).

To provide for variation in learning, pupils may pantomime an abstract word, followed by peers guessing the vocabulary term. An illustration may also be drawn for some of these words which lend themselves to doing this. Pupils must become conscious of developing their very own vocabularies. It is a doorway to success in reading/speaking and life in general.

Words might well be put into appropriate categories, depending upon the unit being taught or academic area stressed. Thus, for example, in a social studies unit emphasizing economics, the following vocabulary terms become important: goods, services, production, distribution, wages and salaries, inflation, market economy, public sector, opportunity costs/ benefits, assembly line, standardized parts, promotion, corporations, cash/credit transactions, mortgages, and loans.

Vocabulary terms should be understood clearly and used in sentences and discussions. With use, the level of application is being stressed in terms of degrees of complexity. Below the level of application or use in decreasing levels of complexity are recall. Certainly, by seeing the above named economic terms in print in initial learnings, the pupil may recall or rehearse subject matter for retention purposes. This is necessary in order to move upward sequentially to more complex learnings in attaching *meaning* to each concept. Opportunities then abound to use in practical written/oral experiences involving the above named economic vocabulary terms. Each vocabulary term may be used in the following ways :

- planning sessions in working on a project

- problem-solving in seeking answers to identified questions
- demonstrations and experiments performed
- literature circle discussions involving library books
- question the author's writings of the library book involving higher levels of cognition
- reciprocal reading experiences (Shepard *et al.* 2007).

IN CONCLUSION

Vocabulary development is important for each pupil. The teacher needs to find innovative ways of assisting learners to achieve vocabulary growth in the listening, speaking, reading, and writing vocabularies. Rich vocabularies are needed in schooling as well as throughout life. For the later work place and for personal enjoyment, vocabulary development in acquiring information is important (Ediger, 2008).

REFERENCES

Baumann, James R, et. al. (2007), "Bumping into Spicy, Tasty Words That Catch Your Tongue;" A Formative Experiment in Vocabulary Instruction, *The Reading Teacher*, 61 (2), 108-123.

Ediger, Marlow (2007), "The Substitute Teacher in Reading Instruction," *The SubJournal*, 8 (2), 67-73.

Ediger, Marlow, and D. Bhaskara Rao (2007), *Language Arts Education*. New Delhi, India: Discovery Publishing House.

Ediger, Marlow (2008), "The Psychology of Parental Involvement in Reading," *Reading Improvement*, 45 (1), 46-52.

Ediger, Marlow (2007), "Learning Activities in the Curriculum," *College Student Journal*, 41 (4), 967-969.

Hawkins, Joanna (2006), "Think Before You Write," *Educational Leadership*, 64 (2), 63-67.

Shepard, *et al.;* 2007), "Inspiring Students to Create The Future," *Phi delta Kappan*, 89 (3), 200-203.

Additional Reading

Amala, P.A. and Anupama, P., Authors and Digumarti Bhaskara Rao, Editor (2004). *History of Education.* New Delhi : Discovery Publishing House. ISBN 81-7141-860-0.

Appala Naidu, P.Ch., Author and Digumarti Bhaskara Rao, Editor (2007). *Student Feedback Methods.* New Delhi : Discovery Publishing House.

Bhaskara Rao, Digumarti (1994). *Scientific Aptitude.* New Delhi : Ashish Publishing House. ISBN 81-7024-658-X.

Bhaskara Rao, Digumarti (1995). *Animal Kingdom.* New Delhi : Discovery Publishing House. ISBN 81-7141-274-2.

Bhaskara Rao, Digumarti (1995). *Batracology.* New Delhi : Discovery Publishing House. ISBN 81-7141-279-3.

Bhaskara Rao, Digumarti (1997). *Scientific Attitude.* New Delhi : Discovery Publishing House. ISBN 81-7141-381-1.

Bhaskara Rao, Digumarti (1996). *Scientific Attitude vis-à-vis Scientific Aptitude.* New Delhi : Discovery Publishing House. ISBN 81-7141-308-0.

Bhaskara Rao, Digumarti (2004). *Scientific Attitude, Scientific Aptitude and Achievement.* New Delhi : Discovery Publishing House. ISBN 81-7141-781-7.

Bhaskara Rao, Digumarti (2004). *Educational Administration.* New Delhi : Discovery Publishing House. ISBN 81-7141-842-2.

Bhaskara Rao, Digumarti (2004). *Issues in School Education.* New Delhi : Discovery Publishing House. ISBN 81-8356-025-3.

Bhaskara Rao, Digumarti, Editor (1996). *Encyclopaedia of Education For All,* 5 Volumes. New Delhi : APH Publishing Corporation. ISBN 81-7024-759-4 (set).

Vol. I *Education For All : The World Conference.* ISBN 81-7024-760-8.

Vol. II *Education For All : The EPA-9 Summit.* ISBN 81-7024-761-6.

Vol. II Education For All : Quality Education For All. ISBN 81-7024-762-6.

Vol. IV Education For All : Planning and Monitoring. ISBN 81-7024-763-4.

Vol. V Education For All : The Indian Scenario. ISBN 81-7024-764-0.

Bhaskara Rao, Digumarti, Editor (1999). *International Encyclopaedia of AIDS*, 11 Volumes. New Delhi: Discovery Publishing House. ISBN 81-7141-522-6 (set).

Vol. 1 *Introduction to HIV/AIDS*. ISBN 81-7141-523-7.

Vol. 2 *HIV/AIDS – Issues and Challenges*, 2 parts. ISBN 81-7141-524-5.

Vol. 3 *HIV/AIDS – Socio Economic Realities*. ISBN 81-7141-524-3.

Vol. 4 *HIV/AIDS – Law Ethics and Human Rights*, 2 parts. ISBN 81-7141-526-1.

Vol. 5 *AIDS and NGOs*. ISBN 81-7141-527-X.

Vol. 6 *AIDS and Home Care*. ISBN 81-7141-528-8.

Vol. 7 *STD Case Management*. ISBN 81-7141-529-6.

Vol. 8 *HIV/AIDS Prevention and Care – Teaching Modules for Nurses and Midwives*. ISBN 81-7141-530-X.

Vol. 9 *HIV Prevention Education for Educational Institutions*. ISBN 81-7141-531-8.

Vol.10 *Instructional Modules for AIDS Education*. ISBN 81-7141-532-6.

Vol.11 *School Health Education to prevent AIDS and STD – A Package for Curriculum Planners*. ISBN 81-7141-533-4.

Bhaskara Rao, Digumarti, Editor (2000). *International Encyclopaedia of Human Rights*, 7 Volumes in 13 Parts. New Delhi : Discovery Publishing House. ISBN 81-7141-567-9 (set).

Vol. 1 *International Instruments of Human Rights*, 2 Parts. ISBN 81-7141-569-4.

Vol. 2 *Regional Instruments of Human Rights*. ISBN 81-7141-604-7.

Vol. 3 *Human Rights and the United Nations*, 2 parts. ISBN 81-7141-605-5.

Vol. 4 *Fact Files of Human Rights*, 3 Parts. ISBN 81-7141-606-3.

Vol. 5 *Study Stories of Human Rights*, 3 parts. ISBN 81-7141-607-3.

Vol. 6 *International Meetings on Human Rights*, 2 parts. ISBN 81-714-608-X.

Vol. 7 *Professional Training in Human Rights*. ISBN 81-7141-609-8.

Bhaskara Rao, Digumarti, Editor (2000). *International Encyclopaedia of Science and Technology Education*, 11 Volumes. New Delhi : Discovery Publishing House. ISBN 81-7141-548-2 (set).

Vol. 1 *Science and Technology Education*. ISBN 81-7141-568-7.

Vol. 2 *Science Education in Developing Countries*. ISBN 81-7141-569-9.

Vol. 3 *Organizational Structure of Science*. ISBN 81-7141-570-9.

Vol. 4 *Science Education in Asia and the Pacific*. ISBN 81-7141-571-7

Vol. 5 *Science and Technology Education For All*. ISBN 81-7141-572-5.

Vol. 6 *Values, Ethics, Talent and Girls in Science and Technology Education*. ISBN 81-7141-573-3.

Vol. 7 *Popularization of Science and Technology Education*. ISBN 81-7141-574-1.

Vol. 8 *Science, Power and Society*. ISBN 81-7141- 575-X.

Vol. 9 *Information Technology*. ISBN 81-7141-576-8.

Vol.10 *Teacher Training in Science and Technology Education*. ISBN 81-7142-577-6.

Vol.11 *Teacher Training in Science and Technology : A Curriculum Framework*. ISBN 81-7141-578-4.

Bhaskara Rao, Digumarti, Editor (2000). *Education For All : Achieving the Goal*, 3 Volumes. New Delhi : APH Publishing Corporation. ISBN 81-7648-152-1 (set).

Vol. I *The Global Consensus*. ISBN 81-7648-155-6.

Vol. II *Mid-Decade Review Reports of Regional Seminars*. ISBN 81-7648-154-8.

Vol. III *Issues and Trends*. ISBN 81-7648-155-6.

Bhaskara Rao, Digumarti, Editor (2004). *International Encyclopaedia of Learning to Live Together*, 4 Volumes. New Delhi : Discovery Publishing House. ISBN 81-7141-848-1.

Vol. 1 *International Conference on Learning to Live Together.*

Vol. 2 *Globalization and Living Together.*

Vol. 3 *Curriculum for Learning to Live Together.*

Vol. 4 *Science Education for the Contemporary Society* .

Bhaskara Rao, Digumarti, Editor (2005). *Encyclopaedia of Education For All*, 3 Volumes. New Delhi : Discovery Publishing House. ISBN 81-7141-647-0 (Set).

Bhaskara Rao, Digumarti, Editor (2007). *Encyclopaedia of Teacher Education*, 4 Volumes. New Delhi : Discovery Publishing House. ISBN 81-8356-306-6 (Set).

Bhaskara Rao, Digumarti, Editor (2007). *Encyclopaedia of Edeucation for Living Together*, 4 Volumes. New Delhi : Discovery Publishing House. ISBN 81-7141-848-1 (Set).

Bhaskara Rao, Digumarti, Editor (1996). *National Policy on Education*, 2 Volumes. New Delhi: Anmol Publications Pvt. Ltd. ISBN 81-7488-323-1.

Bhaskara Rao, Digumarti, Editor (1996). *Global Perceptions on Peace Education*, 3 Volumes. New Delhi : Discovery Publishing House. ISBN 81-7141-319-6.

Bhaskara Rao, Digumarti, Editor (1997). *Education for the 21st Century.* New Delhi : Discovery Publishing House. ISBN 81-7141-389-7.

Bhaskara Rao, Digumarti, Editor (1997). *Reflections on Scientific Attitude.* New Delhi : Discovery Publishing House. ISBN 81-7141-319-6.

Bhaskara Rao, Digumarti, Editor (1997). *Success Story of a Primary Education Project.* New Delhi : APH Publishing Corporation. ISBN 81-7024-850-7.

Bhaskara Rao, Digumarti, Editor (1997). *World Food Summit.* New Delhi : Discovery Publishing House. ISBN 81-7141-386-2.

Bhaskara Rao, Digumarti, Editor (1997). *Care the Child*, 2 Volumes. New Delhi: Discovery Publishing House. ISBN 81-7141-394-3.

Bhaskara Rao, Digumarti, Editor (1998). *Earth Summit*, 2 Volumes. New Delhi : Discovery Publishing House. ISBN 81-7141-435-4.

Bhaskara Rao, Digumarti, Editor (1998). *Adolescence Education.* New Delhi : Discovery Publishing House. ISBN 81-7141-432-X.

Bhaskara Rao, Digumarti, Editor (1998). *Community and School Nutrition Education.* New Delhi : Discovery Publishing House. ISBN 81-7141-435-4.

Bhaskara Rao, Digumarti, Editor (1998). *District Primary Education Programme.* New Delhi: Discovery Publishing House. ISBN 81-7141-396-X.

Bhaskara Rao, Digumarti, Editor (1998). *National Policy on Education : Towards an Enlightened and Humane Society.* New Delhi : Discovery Publishing House. ISBN 81-7141-426-5.

Bhaskara Rao, Digumarti, Editor (1998). *Reforming School Education.* New Delhi : Discovery Publishing House. ISBN 81-7141-403-6.

Bhaskara Rao, Digumarti, Editor (1998). *Teacher Education in India.* New Delhi : Discovery Publishing House. ISBN 81-7141-406-0.

Bhaskara Rao, Digumarti, Editor (1998). *World Summit for Social Development.* New Delhi : Discovery Publishing House. ISBN 81-7141-420-6.

Bhaskara Rao, Digumarti, Editor (2001). *Nuclear Materials : Issues and Concerns*, 2 Volumes. New Delhi : Discovery Publishing House. ISBN 81-7141-611-X.

Bhaskara Rao, Digumarti, Editor (2001). *Distance Education in Different Countries.* New Delhi : APH Publishing Corporation. ISBN 81-7648-229-3.

Bhaskara Rao, Digumarti, Editor (2001). *Decentralised Management of Education : Management of Education in Panchayati Raj and Municipal Bodies.* New Delhi : Discovery Publishing House. ISBN 81-7141-617-9.

Bhaskara Rao, Digumarti, Editor (2001). *Electrochemistry for Environmental Protection.* New Delhi: Discovery Publishing House. ISBN 81-7141-619-5.

Bhaskara Rao, Digumarti, Editor (2001). *Global Educational Studies.* New Delhi : Discovery Publishing House. ISBN 81-7141-616-0.

Bhaskara Rao, Digumarti, Editor (2001). *Global Synthesis of Educational Assessment.* New Delhi : Discovery Publishing House. ISBN 81-7141-613-6.

Bhaskara Rao, Digumarti, Editor (2001). *Jomtein Decade of Education.* New Delhi : Discovery Publishing House. ISBN 81-7141-618-7.

Bhaskara Rao, Digumarti, Editor (2001). *World Conference on Education for All.* New Delhi: APH Publishing Corporation. ISBN 81-7141-274-9.

Bhaskara Rao, Digumarti, Editor (2001). *World Conference on Higher Education.* New Delhi : Discovery Publishing House. ISBN 81-7141-610-1.

Bhaskara Rao, Digumarti, Editor (2001). *World Conference on Science.* New Delhi : Discovery Publishing House. ISBN 81-7141-612-8.

Bhaskara Rao, Digumarti, Editor (2003). *Inspiring Experiences in Teacher Education.* New Delhi : Discovery Publishing House. ISBN 81-7141-656-X.

Bhaskara Rao, Digumarti, Editor (2003). *International Studies in Education*, 3 Volumes. New Delhi : Discovery Publishing House. ISBN 81-7141-647-0.

Bhaskara Rao, Digumarti, Editor (2003). *Military Conversion : Impact on Science and Technology.* New Delhi : Discovery Publishing House. ISBN 81-7141-578-4.

Bhaskara Rao, Digumarti, Editor (2003). *United Nations Millennium Summit.* New Delhi : Discovery Publishing House. ISBN 81-7141-632-2.

Bhaskara Rao, Digumarti, Editor (2003). *World Assembly on Aging.* New Delhi : Discovery Publishing House. ISBN 81-7141-637-3.

Bhaskara Rao, Digumarti, Editor (2003). *World Conference on Human Rights.* New Delhi: Discovery Publishing House. ISBN 81-7141-661-6.

Bhaskara Rao, Digumarti, Editor (2003). *World Education Forum.* New Delhi: Discovery Publishing House. ISBN 81-7141-639-X.

Bhaskara Rao, Digumarti, Editor (2003). *Education, Employment and Human Resource Development*. New Delhi : Discovery Publishing House. ISBN 81-7141- 681-0.

Bhaskara Rao, Digumarti, Editor (2003). *Successful Schooling*. New Delhi : Discovery Publishing House. ISBN 81-7141-677-2.

Bhaskara Rao, Digumarti, Editor (2003). *European Education and Teachers.* New Delhi: Discovery Publishing House. ISBN 81-7141-702-7.

Bhaskara Rao, Digumarti, Editor (2003). *Teachers in a Changing World.* New Delhi : Discovery Publishing House. ISBN 81-7141-694-2.

Bhaskara Rao, Digumarti, Editor (2004). *International Guidelines on Open and Distance Teacher Education*. New Delhi: Discovery Publishing House. ISBN 81-7141-777-9.

Bhaskara Rao, Digumarti, Editor (2004). *Adult Learning in the 21st Century.* New Delhi: Discovery Publishing House. ISBN 81-7141-797-3.

Bhaskara Rao, Digumarti, Editor (2004). *Educational Practices : Research and Recommendations*. New Delhi: Discovery Publishing House. ISBN 81-7141-835-X.

Bhaskara Rao, Digumarti, Editor (2004). *General Secondary Education In the 21st Century*. New Delhi: Discovery Publishing House.

Bhaskara Rao, Digumarti, Editor (2004). *Reforming Secondary Education.* New Delhi: Discovery Publishing House. ISBN 81-7141-843-0.

Bhaskara Rao, Digumarti, Editor (2004). *Human Rights Education.* New Delhi : Discovery Publishing House. ISBN 81-7141-882-1.

Bhaskara Rao, Digumarti, Editor (2004). *United Nations Decade for Human Rights Education.* New Delhi : Discovery Publishing House. ISBN 81-7141- 887-2.

Bhaskara Rao, Digumarti, Editor (2004). *Technical and Vocational Education and Training in the 21st Century.* New Delhi : Discovery Publishing House. ISBN 81-7141-984-4.

Bhaskara Rao, Digumarti, Editor (2005). *Encyclopaedia of Education For All,* 5 Volumes. New Delhi : Discovery Publishing House.

Bhaskara Rao, Digumarti and B.S.V. Dutt, Editors (2003). *Education : Programmes and Policies.* New Delhi : APH Publishing Corporation. ISBN 81-7648-470-9.

Bhaskara Rao, Digumarti, C.A.P. Swamy and B.S.V. Dutt (1997). *Self-Evaluation in Student Teaching*. New Delhi : Discovery Publishing House. ISBN 81-7141-374-9.

Bhaskara Rao, Digumarti and C.D. Swarna Lattha, Editors (2006). *Encyclopaedia of Biotechnology*, 5 Volumes. New Delhi : Discovery Publishing House. ISBN 81-8356-168-3 (set).

Bhaskara Rao, Digumarti, C. Sridevi and K. Vijaya (1995). *Achievement in Social Studies.* New Delhi: Discovery Publishing House. ISBN 81-7141-281-5.

Bhaskara Rao, Digumarti and D. Naresh Kumar (2004). *School Teacher Effectiveness.* New Delhi : Discovery Publishing House. ISBN 81-7141-782-5.

Bhaskara Rao, Digumarti and D. Sridhar (2002). *Job Satisfaction of School Teachers.* New Delhi : Discovery Publishing House. ISBN 81-7141-652-7.

Bhaskara Rao, Digumarti and Digumarti Pushpa Latha, Editors (1998). *International Encyclopaedia of Women*, 5 Volumes. New Delhi : Discovery Publishing House. ISBN 81-7141-410-9 (Set).

Vol. 1 *Status of World's Women*. ISBN 81-7141- 494-X.

Vol. 2 *Women, Education and Empowerment.* ISBN 81-7141-498-1.

Vol. 3 *Women Challenges and Advancement.* ISBN 81-7141-497-4.

Vol. 4 *Women and Family Health.* ISBN 81-7141- 497-4.

Vol. 5 *Women and International Action.* ISBN 81-7141-498-2.

Babu, P.C., Author and Digumarti Bhaskara Rao, Editor (2004). *Flowers of Wisdom.* New Delhi : Discovery Publishing House. ISBN 81-7141-695-0.

Babu, P.C., Author and Digumarti Bhaskara Rao, Editor (2008). *Worlds of Wisdom.* New Delhi: Discovery Publishing House.

Bhagya Lakshmi, L., Author and Digumarti Bhaskara Rao, Editor (2000). *Reading and Comprehension.* New Delhi : Discovery Publishing House. ISBN 81-7141-543-1.

Bhasha, S.A., Author and Digumarti Bhaskara Rao, Editor (2004). *Methods of Teaching Geography.* New Delhi : Discovery Publishing House. ISBN 81-7141-807-4.

Bhaskara Rao, Digumarti (1986). *Dhrushya Sravana Bodhanapakaranalu* (Audio Visual Teaching Aids). Guntur : Nagarjuna Publishers.

Bhaskara Rao, Digumarti (1993). *Jeevasashtra Bodhana* (Teaching of Biology). Guntur : Nagarjuna Publishers.

Bhaskara Rao, Digumarti (1994). *Vidya Manovignana Sastram* (Educational Psychology). Guntur : Nagarjuna Publishers.

Bhaskara Rao, Digumarti (1995). *Vignanasasthra Bodhana* (Teaching of science) Guntur : Nagarjuna Publishers.

Bhaskara Rao, Digumarti (1997). *Vidya Manovignana Sastram* (Educational Psychology). Guntur : Creative Press.

Bhaskara Rao, Digumarti (1998). *DSC Study Material.* Guntur : Nagarjuna Publishers.

Bhaskara Rao, Digumarti (1998). *Upadhyayudu Vidya.* (Teacher and Education) Guntur : Nagarjuna Publishers.

Bhaskara Rao, Digumarti (1998). *Vidya Drukpadalu* (Perspectives of Education). Guntur : Nagarjuna Publishers.

Bhaskara Rao, Digumarti (1999). *EdCET Teaching Aptitude.* Guntur : Nagarjuna Publishers.

Bhaskara Rao, Digumarti (2001). *Bharata Samajamulo Upadyayudu Vidhya* (Teacher and Education in Emerging Indian Society). Guntur : Sri Nagarjuna Publishers.

Bhaskara Rao, Digumarti (2001). *Bhoutika Sastra Bodhana Padhatulu* (Methods of Teaching Physical Science). Guntur : Sri Nagarjuna Publishers.

Bhaskara Rao, Digumarti (2001). *Jeeva Sastra Bodhana Padhatulu* (Methods of Teaching Biology). Guntur : Sri Nagarjuna Publishers.

Bhaskara Rao, Digumarti (2001). *Vidya Manovignana Sastram* (Educational Psychology). Guntur : Sri Nagarjuna Publishers.

Bhaskara Rao, Digumarti (2003). *Patasala Yajamanyam / Paripalana* (School Management and Administration). Guntur : Sri Nagarjuna Publishers.

Bhaskara Rao, Digumarti and A. Jagadish (2009). *Vignansastra Bodhana Padhatulu* (Methods of Teaching Science).Guntur : Sri Nagarjuna Publishers.

Bhaskara Rao, Digumarti and B. Prasad Babu (2009). *Pradhamika Vidya mariyu Vileena Vidya Dhrukpadhalu* (Perspectives in Primary Education and Inclusive Education). Guntur : Sri Nagarjuna Publishers.

Bhaskara Rao, Digumarti and B. Prasad Babu (2009). *Vidya Manovignana Sastram* (Educational Psychology). Guntur : Sri Nagarjuna Publishers.

Bhaskara Rao, Digumarti and D. Naresh Kumar (2004). *School Teacher Effectiveness.* New Delhi : Discovery Publishing House. ISBN 81-7141-782-5.

Bhaskara Rao, Digumarti and Digumarthi Harshitha (2004). *Adjustment of Adolescents.* New Delhi: APH Publishing House. ISBN 81-7648-836-8.

Bhaskara Rao, Digumarti and Digumarthi Harshitha, Editors (2001). *Education in India.* New Delhi: APH Publishing House. ISBN 81-7648-207-2.

Bhaskara Rao, Digumarti and Digumarti Pushpa Latha (1994). *Achievement in Biology.* New Delhi : Discovery Publishing House. ISBN 81-7141-264-5.

Bhaskara Rao, Digumarti and Digumarti Pushpa Latha (1994). *Achievement in Science.* New Delhi : Discovery Publishing House. ISBN 81-7141-280-70.

Bhaskara Rao, Digumarti and Digumarti Pushpa Latha (1995). *Achievement in English.* New Delhi : Discovery Publishing House. ISBN 81-7141-283-1.

Bhaskara Rao, Digumarti and Digumarti Pushpa Latha (1995). *Achievement in Mathematics.* New Delhi : Discovery Publishing House. ISBN 81-7141-278-5.

Bhaskara Rao, Digumarti and Digumarti Pushpa Latha (2004). *Education for Women.* New Delhi : Discovery Publishing House. ISBN 81-7141 873-2.

Bhaskara Rao, Digumarti and E. Sreekanth Babu (2004). *Educational Interests of School Students.* New Delhi : Discovery Publishing House. ISBN 81-7141-837-6.

Bhaskara Rao, Digumarti and G. Prasanthi (2009). *Samardya Nirmanamu* (Capacity Building). Guntur : Sri Nagarjuna Publishers.

Bhaskara Rao, Digumarti and K. Subba Rao (2009). *Elementary Vidya, Pranalika, Yajamanyam, Upadyaya Kartavyalu* (Elementary Education, Planning, Management and Teacher Functions). Guntur : Sri Nagarjuna Publishers.

Bhaskara Rao, Digumarti and K. Vijaya (1995). *A Text Book Evaluation.* Ambala Cantt : The Associated Publishers.

Bhaskara Rao, Digumarti and K.R.S. Sambasiva Rao, Editors (1996). *Current Trends in Indian Education.* New Delhi : Discovery Publishing House. ISBN 81-7141-311-0.

Bhaskara Rao, Digumarti and M.A. Fayaz (2004). *Problems of Primary School Drop-outs.* New Delhi : Discovery Publishing House. ISBN 81-7141- 834-1.

Bhaskara Rao, Digumarti and N.V.M. Mohana Rao (2002). *Problems of Mentally Handicapped Children.* New Delhi : Discovery Publishing House. ISBN 81-7141- 645-4.

Bhaskara Rao, Digumarti and S. Chandra Mohan (2002). *Sports Management.* New Delhi : APH Publishing House. ISBN 81-7648-467-9.

Bhaskara Rao, Digumarti and S.A. Khader (2004). *Problems of Private School Teachers.* New Delhi : Discovery Publishing Corporation. ISBN 81-7141-838-4.

Bhaskara Rao, Digumarti and S.A. Khader (2004). *School Education in India.* New Delhi : Discovery Publishing Corporation. ISBN 81-7141-849-X.

Bhaskara Rao, Digumarti and Sk. Johni Basha (2004). *Teachers' Population Education Awareness.* New Delhi : Discovery Publishing House. ISBN 81-7141-832-5.

Bhaskara Rao, Digumarti, Digumarthi Harshitha and K.R.S. Sambasiva Rao, Editors (1999). *Advanced Biotechnology.* New Delhi : Discovery Publishing House. ISBN 81-7141-516-4.

Bhaskara Rao, Digumarti, Digumarti Pushpa Latha and Digumarthi Harshitha, Editors (2001). *Biological Warfare.* New Delhi: Discovery Publishing House. ISBN 81-7141-597-0.

Bhaskara Rao, Digumarti, Digumarti Pushpa Latha and Digumarthi Harshitha, Editors (2001). *Women as Educators.* New Delhi: Discovery Publishing House. ISBN 81-7141-602-0.

Bhaskara Rao, Digumarti, Digumarti Pushpa Latha and Digumarthi Harshitha, Editors (2001). *Assessing Learning Achievement.* New Delhi: Discovery Publishing House. ISBN 81-7141-601-2.

Bhaskara Rao, Digumarti, Digumarti Pushpa Latha and Digumarthi Harshitha, Editors (2001). *Energy Security.* New Delhi : Discovery Publishing House. ISBN 81-7141-598-9.

Bhaskara Rao, Digumarti, Editor (2010). *Elementary Vidya, Pranalika, Yajamanyam, Upadyaya Kartavyalu – Question Bank* (Elementary Education, Planning, Management and Teacher Functions). Guntur: Sri Nagarjuna Publishers.

Bhaskara Rao, Digumarti, Editor (2010). *Ganithasastra Bodhana Padhatulu – Question Bank* (Methods of Teaching Science).Guntur : Sri Nagarjuna Publishers.

Bhaskara Rao, Digumarti, Editor (2010). *Methods of Teaching English – Question Bank.* Guntur : Sri Nagarjuna Publishers.

Bhaskara Rao, Digumarti, Editor (2010). *Pradhamika Vidya mariyu Vileena Vidya Dhrukpadhalu – Question Bank* (Perspectives in Primary Education and Inclusive Education). Guntur : Sri Nagarjuna Publishers.

Bhaskara Rao, Digumarti, Editor (2010). *Samardya Nirmanamu – Question Bank* (Capacity Building). Guntur : Sri Nagarjuna Publishers.

Bhaskara Rao, Digumarti, Editor (2010). *Sanghikasastra Bodhana Padhatulu – Question Bank* (Methods of Teaching Social Studies).Guntur : Sri Nagarjuna Publishers.

Bhaskara Rao, Digumarti, Editor (2010). *Telugu Bodhana Padhatulu – Question Bank* (Methods of Teaching Social Studies).Guntur: Sri Nagarjuna Publishers.

Bhaskara Rao, Digumarti, Editor (2010). *Vidya Manovignana Sastram – Question Bank* (Educational Psychology). Guntur : Sri Nagarjuna Publishers.

Bhaskara Rao, Digumarti, Editor (2010). *Vignansastra Bodhana Padhatulu – Question Bank* (Methods of Teaching Science).Guntur : Sri Nagarjuna Publishers.

Bhaskara Rao, Digumarti, N. Saraja, J. Lalitha and V. Mrunalini, Translators (2008). *Vidya – Samajam (Education - Society). Hyderabad* : Dr. B.R. Ambedkar Open University.

Bhaskara Rao, Digumarti, V.V. Rao, V.V. Lakshmi and V.V. Krishna, Editors (1999). *Status and Advancement of Women.* New Delhi: APH Publishing Corporation. ISBN 81-7648-169-6.

Bhuvaneswara Lakshmi, G. and K. Subba Rao, Authors and Digumarti Bhaskara Rao, Editor (2004). *Methods of Teaching Biology.* New Delhi : Discovery Publishing House. ISBN 81-7141-914-3.

Bhuvaneswara Lakshmi, G., Author and Digumarti Bhaskara Rao, Editor (2004). *Methods of Teaching Life Science.* New Delhi : Discovery Publishing House. ISBN 81-7141-804-X.

Bhuvaneswara Lakshmi, Gadde, Author and Digumarti Bhaskara Rao, Editor(2000). *Attitude Towards Science.* New Delhi: Discovery Publishing House. ISBN 81-7141-541-6.

Bujji Babu, K., Author and Digumarti Bhaskara Rao, Editor (2007). *Teaching Aptitude of Primary School Teachers.* New Delhi: Sonali Publications. ISBN 81-8411-083-9.

Chary, K.V.N.B., Author and Digumarti Bhaskara Rao, Editor (2006). *Techniques of Teaching Physics.* New Delhi : Sonali Publications. ISBN 81-8411-046-4.

Chowdary, S.B.J.R. and Naga Raju, Authors and Digumarti Bhaskara Rao, Editor (2004). *Mastery of Teaching Skills.* New Delhi : Discovery Publishing House. ISBN 81-7141-861-9.

Dayakara Reddy, V. and Digumarti Bhaskara Rao, Editors (2006). *Value-Oriented Education.* New Delhi : Discovery Publishing House. ISBN 81-8356-051-2.

Devraj, T.A.S., Author and Digumarti Bhaskara Rao, Editor (1997). *Trace Analysis of Uranium and Thorium.* New Delhi : Discovery Publishing House. ISBN 81-7141-375-7.

Digumarti Bhaskara Rao and M. Srihari (2009). *Vardamana Bharata Desamulo Vidya* (Education in Emerging India). Guntur : Sri Nagarjuna Publishers.

Digumarti Bhaskara Rao, Editor (2010). *Vardamana Bharata Desamulo Vidya – Question Bank* (Education in Emerging India). Guntur : Sri Nagarjuna Publishers.

Durga Rani, K., Author and Digumarti Bhaskara Rao, Editor (2000). *Educational Aspirations and Scientific Attitudes.* New Delhi : Discovery Publishing House. ISBN 81-7141-555-5.

Dutt, B.S.V. and Digumarti Bhaskara Rao (2001). *Empowering Primary Teachers.* New Delhi : Discovery Publishing House. ISBN 81-7141-615-2.

Dutt, B.S.V., Author and Digumarti Bhaskara Rao, Editor (2004). *Comparative Education.* New Delhi: Discovery Publishing House. ISBN 81-7141-912-7.

Ediger, Marlow and Digumarti Bhaskara Rao (1996). *Science Curriculum.* New Delhi: Discovery Publishing House. ISBN 81-7141-321-8.

Ediger, Marlow and Digumarti Bhaskara Rao (2000). *Teaching Mathematics Successfully.* New Delhi : Discovery Publishing House. ISBN 81-7141-552-0.

Ediger, Marlow and Digumarti Bhaskara Rao (2001). *Teaching Science Successfully.* New Delhi : Discovery Publishing House. ISBN 81-7141-600-4.

Ediger, Marlow and Digumarti Bhaskara Rao (2001). *Teaching Social Studies Successfully.* New Delhi : Discovery Publishing House. ISBN 81-7141-596-2.

Ediger, Marlow and Digumarti Bhaskara Rao (2002). *Elementary Curriculum.* New Delhi : Discovery Publishing House. ISBN 81-7141-658-6.

Ediger, Marlow and Digumarti Bhaskara Rao (2002). *Improving School Administration.* New Delhi : Discovery Publishing House. ISBN 81-7141-633-0

Ediger, Marlow and Digumarti Bhaskara Rao (2002). *Philosophy and Curriculum.* New Delhi: Discovery Publishing House. ISBN 81-7141-631-4.

Ediger, Marlow and Digumarti Bhaskara Rao (2003). *Elementary Curriculum Improvement.* New Delhi : Discovery Publishing House. ISBN 81-7141-740-X.

Ediger, Marlow and Digumarti Bhaskara Rao (2003). *Language Arts Curriculum.* New Delhi : Discovery Publishing House. ISBN 81-7141-657-8.

Ediger, Marlow and Digumarti Bhaskara Rao (2003). *Psychology and Curriculum.* New Delhi : Discovery Publishing House. ISBN 81-7141-691-8.

Ediger, Marlow and Digumarti Bhaskara Rao (2003). *School Curriculum and Administration.* New Delhi : Discovery Publishing House. ISBN 81-7141-709-4.

Ediger, Marlow and Digumarti Bhaskara Rao (2003). *School Curriculum and Administration.* New Delhi : Discovery Publishing House. ISBN 81-7141-709-4.

Ediger, Marlow and Digumarti Bhaskara Rao (2003). *Teaching Language Arts Successfully.* New Delhi : Discovery Publishing House. ISBN 81-7141-678-0.

Ediger, Marlow and Digumarti Bhaskara Rao (2003). *Teaching Mathematics in Elementary Schools.* New Delhi : Discovery Publishing House. ISBN 81-7141-687-X.

Ediger, Marlow and Digumarti Bhaskara Rao (2003). *Teaching Science in Elementary Schools.* New Delhi: Discovery Publishing House. ISBN 81-7141-698-5.

Ediger, Marlow and Digumarti Bhaskara Rao (2004). *Relevancy in Elementary Curriculum.* New Delhi : Discovery Publishing House. ISBN 81-7141-845-9.

Ediger, Marlow and Digumarti Bhaskara Rao (2004). *School Organisation.* New Delhi : Discovery Publishing House. ISBN 81-7141-843-0.

Ediger, Marlow and Digumarti Bhaskara Rao (2005). *Quality School Education.* New Delhi : Discovery Publishing House. ISBN 81-8356-022-9.

Ediger, Marlow and Digumarti Bhaskara Rao (2006). *Administration of Schools.* New Delhi : Discovery Publishing House.

Ediger, Marlow and Digumarti Bhaskara Rao (2006). *Community College – Curriculum and Teaching.* New Delhi : Discovery Publishing House. ISBN 81-8356-053-9.

Ediger, Marlow and Digumarti Bhaskara Rao (2006). *Curriculum of School Subjects.* New Delhi : Discovery Publishing House.

Ediger, Marlow and Digumarti Bhaskara Rao (2006). *Curriculum Organisation.* New Delhi: Discovery Publishing House.

Ediger, Marlow and Digumarti Bhaskara Rao (2006). *Issues in School Curruculum.* New Delhi : Discovery Publishing House. ISBN 81-8356-052-0.

Ediger, Marlow and Digumarti Bhaskara Rao (2006). *Reading Curriculum and Instruction.* New Delhi : Discovery Publishing House.

Ediger, Marlow and Digumarti Bhaskara Rao (2006). *Successful School Education.* New Delhi : Discovery Publishing House. ISBN 81-8356-054-7.

Ediger, Marlow and Digumarti Bhaskara Rao (2006). *Successful School Administration.* New Delhi : Discovery Publishing House. ISBN 81-8356-046-6.

Ediger, Marlow and Digumarti Bhaskara Rao (2007). *Language Arts Education.* New Delhi : Discovery Publishing House. ISBN 81-8356-333-3.

Ediger, Marlow and Digumarti Bhaskara Rao (2007). *School Science Education.* New Delhi : Discovery Publishing House. ISBN 81-8356-352-X.

Ediger, Marlow and Digumarti Bhaskara Rao (2010). *Effective Schooling.* New Delhi : Discovery Publishing House. ISBN 978-81-8356-613-1.

Ediger, Marlow and Digumarti Bhaskara Rao (2010). *Effective School Curriculum.* New Delhi : Discovery Publishing House. ISBN 978-81-8356-585-1.

Ediger, Marlow and Digumarti Bhaskara Rao (2010). *Essays on Teaching Science.* New Delhi : Discovery Publishing House.

Ediger, Marlow and Digumarti Bhaskara Rao (2010). *Essays on Teaching Social Studies.* New Delhi : Discovery Publishing House.

Ediger, Marlow and Digumarti Bhaskara Rao (2010). *Essays on Teaching Reading.* New Delhi : Discovery Publishing House.

Ediger, Marlow and Digumarti Bhaskara Rao (2010). *Essays on Teaching Mathematics.* New Delhi : Discovery Publishing House.

Ediger, Marlow and Digumarti Bhaskara Rao (2010). *Essays on Teaching and Learning.* New Delhi : Discovery Publishing House.

Ediger, Marlow and Digumarti Bhaskara Rao, Editors (2006). *Encyclopaedia of School Education*, 5 Volumes. New Delhi : Discovery Publishing House. ISBN 81-8356-308-2 (set).

Ediger, Marlow and Digumarti Bhaskara Rao, Editors (2006). *Encyclopaedia of School Administration*, 4 Volumes. New Delhi : Discovery Publishing House. ISBN 81-8356-307-4 (set).

Ediger, Marlow and Digumarti Bhaskara Rao, Editors (2007). *Encyclopaedia of School Curriculum*, 10 Volumes. New Delhi : Discovery Publishing House. ISBN 81-8356-305-8 (set).

Ediger, Marlow and Digumarti Bhaskara Rao, Editors (2007). *Encyclopaedia of Teaching*, 8 Volumes. New Delhi : Discovery Publishing House. ISBN 81-8356-305-8 (set).

Ediger, Marlow, B.S.V. Dutt and Digumarti Bhaskara Rao (2003). *Teaching English Successfully.* New Delhi : Discovery Publishing House. ISBN 81-7141-707-8.

Elizabeth, M.E.S., Author and Digumarti Bhaskara Rao, Editor (2004). *Methods of Teaching English.* New Delhi : Discovery Publishing House. ISBN 81-7141-809-0.

Elizabeth, M.E.S., Author and Digumarti Bhaskara Rao, Editor (2004). *Acquisition of English Vocabulary.* New Delhi : Discovery Publishing House. ISBN 81-8356-075-X.

Fatima, Sk. and Digumarti Bhaskara Rao (2008). *Reasoning Ability of Adolescent Students.* New Delhi : Sonali Publications.

Fatima, Sk. Author and Digumarti Bhaskara Rao, Editor (2007). *Reasoning Ability of School Students.* New Delhi : Discovery Publishing House. ISBN 81-8356-330-9.

G.E.P. Sastry and G. Satya Narayana, Authors, Bhaskara Rao, Digumarti, Editor (2009). *Sanghikasastra Bodhana Padhatulu* (Methods of Teaching Social Studies).Guntur : Sri Nagarjuna Publishers.

Gopala Krishna, G., A. Rama Krishna, K. Subba Rao and Bhaskara Rao, Digumarti (2004). *Jeevasashtra Bodhana Padhatulu* (Methods of Teaching of Biological science). Guntur : Sri Nagarjuna Publishers.

Gopala Krishna, M., Author and Digumarti Bhaskara Rao, Editor (2007). *Techniques of Teaching Physical Education.* New Delhi : Sonali Publications. ISBN 81-8411-044-8.

Gopala Krishna, M., Author and Digumarti Bhaskara Rao, Editor (2007). *Techniques of Teaching Education.* New Delhi : Sonali Publications. ISBN 81-8411-062-6.

Harshitha, Digumarthi, Author and Digumarti Bhaskara Rao, Editor (2004). *Methods of Teaching Information Technology.* New Delhi : Discovery Publishing House. ISBN 81-7141-805-8.

Harshitha, Digumarthi, Author and Digumarti Bhaskara Rao, Editor (2007). *Techniques of Teaching Computer Science.* New Delhi : Sonali Publications. ISBN 81-8411-036-7.

Indira Devi, Author and J. Prasanth Kumar and Digumarti Bhaskara Rao, Editors (2004). *Values in Language Text Books.* New Delhi : Discovery Publishing House. ISBN 81-7141-833-3.

Jalaja Kumari, C., Author and Digumarti Bhaskara Rao, Editor (2004). *Methods of Teaching Educational Technology.* New Delhi : Discovery Publishing House. ISBN 81-7141-810-4.

Jalaja Kumari, C., Author and Digumarti Bhaskara Rao, Editor (2007). *Job Satisfaction of Teachers.* New Delhi : Discovery Publishing House.

Janardhan Reddy, B., Author and Digumarti Bhaskara Rao, Editor (2006). *Techniques of Teaching Sociology.* New Delhi : Sonali Publications. ISBN 81-8411-042-1.

Jayasree, K., Author and Digumarti Bhaskara Rao, Editor (1999). *Correlates of Socialisation.* New Delhi : Discovery Publishing House. ISBN 81-7141-517-2.

Jayasree, K., Author and Digumarti Bhaskara Rao, Editor (2004). *Methods of Teaching Science.* New Delhi : Discovery Publishing House. ISBN 81-7141-801-5.

John Babu, C., Author and T.J.R. Prasad, G.M. Madhukar and Digumarti Bhaskara Rao, Editors (2004). *Problem Solving in Mathematics.* New Delhi : APH Publishing Corporation. ISBN 81-7648-273-0.

Joseph Raju, B and G.A. Anitha, Authors and Digumarti Bhaskara Rao, Editor (2004). *Population Education.* New Delhi : Sonali Publications. ISBN 81-88836-31-3.

Krishna Murthy, V., K.S. Sudheer Reddy and Digumarti Bhaskara Rao (2004). *Vidya Manovignana Sastra Adharalu* (Foundations of Educational Psychology). Guntur : Sri Nagarjuna Publishers.

Krishna, G., Author and Digumarti Bhaskara Rao, Editor (2006). *Techniques of Teaching Physical Education.* New Delhi : Discovery Publishing House. ISBN 81-8411-044-8.

Kumar Raja, G., Author and Digumarti Bhaskara Rao, Editor (2007). *Principles of Primary School.* New Delhi : Sonali Publications. ISBN 81-8411-054-5.

Lakshmi Kumari, V., Author and Digumarti Bhaskara Rao, Editor (2006). *Techniques of Teaching Home Science.* New Delhi : Discovery Publishing House. ISBN 81-8411-048-0.

Lalini, V., V. Dayakara Reddy, M. Srihari and Digumarti Bhaskara Rao (2004). *Vidya Adharalu* (Foundations of Education). Guntur : Sri Nagarjuna Publishers.

Lalitha, T., Author and K.S. Prabhakaram, D.S.N. Sastry and Digumarti Bhaskara Rao, Editors (2004). *Educational Philosophic Beliefs.* New Delhi: Discovery Publishing House. ISBN 81-7141-765-5.

Madhava, K., Author and Digumarti Bhaskara Rao, Editor (2008). *Personality of Adolescent Students.* New Delhi: Sonali Publications.

Madhu Bala, Jampala, Author and Digumarti Bhaskara Rao, Editor (2004). *Methods of Teaching Exceptional Children.* New Delhi: Discovery Publishing House. ISBN 81-7141-802-3.

Madhu Bala, Jampala, Author and Digumarti Bhaskara Rao, Editor (2007). *Adjustment, Achievement Motivation and Academic Achievement of Hearing Impaired Students.* New Delhi: Discovery Publishing House

Marja, Talvi and Digumarti Bhaskara Rao, Editors (1996). *Educational Leadership and Social Changes.* New Delhi : Discovery Publishing House. ISBN 81-7141-320-X.

Marlow Ediger and Digumarti Bhaskara Rao, Editors (2006). *Encyclopaedia of School Education*, 5 Volumes. New Delhi : Discovery Publishing House. ISBN 81-8356-308-2 (Set).

Marlow Ediger and Digumarti Bhaskara Rao, Editors (2006). *Encyclopaedia of School Administration*, 4 Volumes. New Delhi : Discovery Publishing House. ISBN 81-8356-307-4 (set).

Marlow Ediger and Digumarti Bhaskara Rao, Editors (2007). *Encyclopaedia of School Curriculum*, 10 Volumes. New Delhi : Discovery Publishing House. ISBN 81-8356-305-8 (set).

Marlow Ediger and Digumarti Bhaskara Rao, Editors (2007). *Encyclopaedia of Teaching*, 8 Volumes. New Delhi : Discovery Publishing House. ISBN 81-8356-305-8 (set).

Naga Kumari, U., Author and Digumarti Bhaskara Rao, Editor (2008). *Science Process Skills of School Students*. New Delhi : Sonali Publications.

Nageswara Rao, S. and M. Srihari, Authors and Digumarti Bhaskara Rao, Editor (2004). *Guidance and Counselling*. New Delhi : Discovery Publishing House. ISBN 81-7141-840-6.

Nageswara Rao, S. and P. Sridhar, Authors and Digumarti Bhaskara Rao, Editor (2004). *Methods and Techniques of Teaching*. New Delhi : Sonali Publications. ISBN 81-88836-33-8.

Nageswara Rao, S., Author and Digumarti Bhaskara Rao, Editor (2006). *Techniques of Teaching Psychology*. New Delhi : Discovery Publishing House. ISBN 81-8411-040-5.

Nirmala Jyothi, M., Author and Digumarti Bhaskara Rao, Editor (2003). *Non-detention System in School Education*. New Delhi : Discovery Publishing House. ISBN 81-7141-654-3.

Padma Tulasi, G., Author and Digumarti Bhaskara Rao, Editor (2004). *Methods of Teaching Elementary Science*. New Delhi : Discovery Publishing House. ISBN 81-7141-871-6.

Pala Prasada Rao, V., Author and D. Bhaskara Rao, Editors (2008). *Functioning of Autonomous Colleges*. New Delhi : Sonali Publications.

Pala Prasada Rao, V., Author and K. N. Rani and D. Bhaskara Rao, Editors (2004).*India Pakistan : Partition Perspectives in Indo English Novels*. New Delhi: Discovery Publishing House. ISBN 81-7141-871-6.

Pitchi Reddy, M., Author and Digumarti Bhaskara Rao, Editor (2007). *Techniques of Teaching Social Sciences*. New Delhi : Sonali Publications. ISBN 81-8411-066-X.

Prabhakaram, K.S., Author and Digumarti Bhaskara Rao, Editors (1998). *Concept Attainment Model in Mathematics Teaching*. New Delhi : Discovery Publishing House. ISBN 81-7141-424-9.

Prasad Babu, B., Author and M.V.R. Raju and Digumarti Bhaskara Rao, Editors (2006). *Behavioural Problems of School Children*. New Delhi: Discovery Publishing House. ISBN 81-8356-206-X.

Prasad Babu, B., Author and P. Madhu and Digumarti Bhaskara Rao, Editors (2006). *Psychological Adjustment and Well-being*. New Delhi: Discovery Publishing House. ISBN 81-8356-204-3.

Prasanth Kumar, J., Author and Digumarti Bhaskara Rao, Editor (1998). *Effectiveness of Distance Education System*. New Delhi : Discovery Publishing House. ISBN 81-7141-437-0.

Prasanth Kumar, J., Author and Digumarti Bhaskara Rao, Editor (2004). *Methods of Teaching Civics*. New Delhi : Discovery Publishing House. ISBN 81-7141-806-6.

Prasanth Kumar, J., Author and G. Sundara Rao and Digumarti Bhaskara Rao, Editors (2000). *Open University Student Support Services*. New Delhi : Discovery Publishing House. ISBN 81-7141-550-4.

Raja Kumari, M.A. and D.R.S. Sundari, Authors and Digumarti Bhaskara Rao, Editor (2004). *Special Education*. New Delhi : Discovery Publishing House. ISBN 81-7141-846-5.

Raja Kumari, M.A. and D.R.S. Sundari, Authors and Digumarti Bhaskara Rao, Editor (2004). *Methods of Teaching Educational Psychology*. New Delhi : Discovery Publishing House. ISBN 81-7141-820-1.

Rama Krishna Prasad and P. Vide Sagar, Authors and Digumarti Bhaskara Rao, Editor (2004). *Methods of Teaching Physical Education*. New Delhi: Discovery Publishing House.

Rama Krishnaiah, D., Author and Digumarti Bhaskara Rao, Editor (1998). *Job Satisfaction of College Teachers*. New Delhi : Discovery Publishing House. ISBN 81-7141-438-9.

Rama Kumar Ratnam, M.V., Author and Digumarti Bhaskara Rao, Editor (1998). *Dukkha : Suffering in Early Buddhism*. New Delhi: Discovery Publishing House. ISBN 81-7141-653-5.

Rama Seshaiah, P. Author and Digumarti Bhaskara Rao, Editor (2004). *Methods of Teaching Home Science*. New Delhi : Discovery Publishing House. ISBN 81-7141-916-X.

Rama Swamy, K., Author and Digumarti Bhaskara Rao, Editor (2007). *Techniques of Teaching Environmental Science*. New Delhi : Sonali Publications. ISBN 81-8411-035-9.

Ramatulasamma, K., Author and Digumarti Bhaskara Rao, Editor (2002). *Job Satisfaction of Teacher Educators.* New Delhi : Discovery Publishing House. ISBN 81-7141-655-1.

Ramesh, A.R., Author and Digumarti Bhaskara Rao, Editor (2006). *Techniques of Teaching Commerce.* New Delhi : Sonali Publications. ISBN 81-8411-043-X.

Ramesh, Ghanta and Digumarti Bhaskara Rao, Editors (1998). *Environmental Education : Problems and Prospects.* New Delhi: Discovery Publishing House. ISBN 81-7141-423-0.

Ranga Rao, B., Author and Digumarti Bhaskara Rao, Editor (2007). *Techniques of Teaching Economics.* New Delhi : Sonali Publications. ISBN 81-8411-056-1.

Ranga Rao, R., Author and Digumarti Bhaskara Rao, Editor (2004). *Methods of Teacher Teaching.* New Delhi : Discovery Publishing House. ISBN 81-7141-812-0.

Rani, S.S., Author and Digumarti Bhaskara Rao, Editor (2006). *Techniques of Teaching Botany.* New Delhi : Discovery Publishing House. ISBN 81-8411-037-5.

Rathaiah, Lavu and Digumarti Bhaskara Rao (1997). *Achievement Correlates.* New Delhi: Discovery Publishing House. ISBN 81-7141-385-4.

Rathaiah, Lavu and Digumarti Bhaskara Rao, Editors (1996), *International Innovations in Education.* New Delhi : Discovery Publishing House. ISBN 81-7141-359-5.

Ravi Krishna, M., Author and Digumarti Bhaskara Rao, Editor (2004). *Examination System.* New Delhi : Discovery Publishing House. ISBN 81-7141-824-4.

Ravi Kumar, M., Author and Digumarti Bhaskara Rao, Editor (2004). *Methods of Teaching Computer Science.* New Delhi : Discovery Publishing House. ISBN 81-7141-823-6.

Rudramamba, B. and V. Lakshmi Kumari, Authors and Digumarti Bhaskara Rao, Editor (2004). *Methods of Teaching Economics.* New Delhi : Discovery Publishing House. ISBN 81-7141-900-3.

Rudramamba, B., Author and Digumarti Bhaskara Rao, Editor (2003). *Problems of Teaching.* New Delhi : APH Publishing Corporation. ISBN 81-7648-462-8.

Sambasiva Rao, P., Author and Digumarti Bhaskara Rao, Editor (2007). *Techniques of Teaching Psychology.* New Delhi : Sonali Publications. ISBN 81-8411-040-5.

Sanjeeva Rao, P.C., Author and Digumarti Bhaskara Rao, Editor (1996). *A Text Book of Geology.* New Delhi : Discovery Publishing House. ISBN 81-7141-313-7.

Santhanam, T., B. Prasad Babu and S. Sugandhi, Authors and Digumarti Bhaskara Rao, Editor (2007). *Children with Learning Disabilities.* New Delhi : Sonali Publications. ISBN 81-8411-077-4.

Santhanam, T., B. Prasad Babu and S. Sugandhi, Authors and Digumarti Bhaskara Rao, Editor (2008). *Learning Disabilities and Remedial Programmes.* New Delhi : Discovery Publishing House.

Sarala, M.M.O., Author and Digumarti Bhaskara Rao, Editor (2006). *Techniques of Teaching English.* New Delhi : Sonali Publications. ISBN 81-8411-047-2.

Satya Narayana, G., Author and Digumarti Bhaskara Rao, Editor (2008). *Attitude towards Social Studies and Achievement in Social Studies.* New Delhi : Sonali Publications.

Satya Narayana, P.V.V. and G. Krishna, Authors and Digumarti Bhaskara Rao, Editor (2004). *Curriculum Development and Management.* New Delhi : Discovery Publishing House. ISBN 81-7141-813-9.

Satya Narayana, V., Author and Digumarti Bhaskara Rao, Editor (2001). *Physical Education, Social Attitudes and Leadership Qualities.* New Delhi: Discovery Publishing House. ISBN 81-7141-593-8.

Shamsuddin, Sk. and V. Dayakara Reddy, Authors and Digumarti Bhaskara Rao, Editor (2007). *Academic Achievement and Values.* New Delhi : Discovery Publishing House.

Singh, Y.C., Author and Digumarti Bhaskara Rao, Editor (2006). *Techniques of Teaching Science.* New Delhi : Sonali Publications. ISBN 81-8411-041-3.

Sirisha Rani, S., Author and Digumarti Bhaskara Rao, Editor (2007). *Techniques of Teaching Botany.* New Delhi : Sonali Publications. ISBN 81-8411-037-5.

Siva Lakshmi, G.V. and G.L. Subbaiah, Authors and Digumarti Bhaskara Rao, Editor (2004). *Methods of Teaching Environmental Science.* New Delhi: Discovery Publishing House. ISBN 81-7141-839-2.

Sivaratnam Reddy, M., Author and Digumarti Bhaskara Rao, Editor (2004). *Creativity in College Students.* New Delhi : Discovery Publishing House. ISBN 81-7141-697-7.

Srihari, M., Author and Digumarti Bhaskara Rao, Editor (2003). *Values of Prospective Teachers.* New Delhi : Discovery Publishing House. ISBN 81-8356-328-7.

Srinivas Rao, P., Author and Digumarti Bhaskara Rao, Editor (2007). *Principles of Secondary School.* New Delhi : Sonali Publications. ISBN 81-8411-058-8.

Srinivas, G. and Digumarti Bhaskara Rao (2007). *Anxiety of Prospective Teachers.* New Delhi : Sonali Publications. ISBN 81-8411-084-7.

Srinivas, M. and I. Prasada Rao, Authors and Digumarti Bhaskara Rao, Editor (2004). *Methods of Teaching History.* New Delhi : Discovery Publishing House. ISBN 81-7141-803-1.

Srinivasa Rao, Mandalapu, Author and Digumarti Bhaskara Rao, Editor (2003). *Achievement Motivation and Achievement in Mathematics.* New Delhi : Discovery Publishing House. ISBN 81-7141-674-8.

Srinivasulu Reddy, M. and K.R.S. Sambasiva Rao, Authors and Digumarti Bhaskara Rao, Editor (1999). *A Text Book of Aquaculture.* New Delhi : Discovery Publishing House. ISBN 81-7141-482-6.

Subba Rao, K., Author and Digumarti Bhaskara Rao, Editor (2007). *School Education Policy.* New Delhi : Discovery Publishing House. ISBN 81-8356-285-X.

Subba Rao, K., Author and Digumarti Bhaskara Rao, Editor (2007). *Education Planning.* New Delhi : Sonali Publications. ISBN 81-8411-053-7.

Subba Rao, K.P., P. Ayodhya and Digumarti Bhaskara Rao (2004). *Patasala Yajamanyam – Vidhya Vyavasthalu* (School Management and Systems of Education). Guntur : Sri Nagarjuna Publishers.

Sudhakar Reddy, Y., Author and Digumarti Bhaskara Rao, Editor (2003). *Creativity in Adolescents.* New Delhi : Discovery Publishing House. ISBN 81-7141-659-4.

Sudhakar, V., B. Ravindra Babu, D.S. Kumar and Digumarti Bhaskara Rao (2004). *Vidya Sanketika Sastram - Computer Vidhya* (Educational Technology and Computer Education). Guntur : Sri Nagarjuna Publishers.

Suneetha, G., Author and Digumarti Bhaskara Rao, Editor (2004). *Environmental Awareness of School Students.* New Delhi : Sonali Publications. ISBN 81-8411-085-5.

Sunil Kumar, K. and K. Rama Krishana, Authors and Digumarti Bhaskara Rao, Editor (2004). *Methods of Teaching Chemistry.* New Delhi : Discovery Publishing House. ISBN 81-7141-913-5.

Sunita, E. and R. Sambasiva Rao, Authors and Digumarti Bhaskara Rao, Editor (2004). *Methods of Teaching Mathematics.* New Delhi : Discovery Publishing House. ISBN 81-7141-915-1.

Surya Madhava, I., Author and Digumarti Bhaskara Rao, Editor (2006). *Techniques of Teaching Geography.* New Delhi : Discovery Publishing House. ISBN 81-8411-034-0.

Surya Madhava, I., Author and Digumarti Bhaskara Rao, Editor (2007). *Techniques of Teaching Political Science.* New Delhi : Discovery Publishing House. ISBN 81-8411-061-8.

Swamy, K.R., Author and Digumarti Bhaskara Rao, Editor (2006). *Techniques of Teaching Environmental Science.* New Delhi : Discovery Publishing House. ISBN 81-8411-035-9.

Swarna Jyothi, K., Author and Digumarti Bhaskara Rao, Editor (2007). *Educational Research.* New Delhi : Sonali Publications. ISBN 81-8411-063-4.

Swarna Latha, C.D., and Digumarti Bhaskara Rao, Editors (2006). *Encyclopaedia of Biotechnology,* 5 Volumes. New Delhi : Discovery Publishing House. ISBN 81-8356-168-3.

Swarupa Rani, T. and J.R. Priyadarshini, Authors and Digumarti Bhaskara Rao, Editor (2004). *Educational Measurement and Evaluation.* New Delhi: Discovery Publishing House. ISBN 81-7141-859-7.

Valeri V. Koustiouk, Author and Digumarti Bhaskara Rao, Editor (2002). *A Text Book of Cryogenics.* New Delhi : Discovery Publishing House. ISBN 81-7141-642-X.

Vamsi Krishna, V., Author and Digumarti Bhaskara Rao, Editor (2004). *School Psychology.* New Delhi: Discovery Publishing House. ISBN 81-7141-880-5.

Vanaja, M. and N. Sneha Latha, Authors and Digumarti Bhaskara Rao, Editor (2004). *Student Shyness.* New Delhi : APH Publishing Corporation.

Vanaja, M., Author and Digumarti Bhaskara Rao, Editor (1999). *Inquiry Training Model.* New Delhi : Discovery Publishing House. ISBN 81-7141-515-6.

Vanaja, M., Author and Digumarti Bhaskara Rao, Editor (2004). *Methods of Teaching Physics.* New Delhi : Discovery Publishing House. ISBN 81-7141-867-8

Veena Kumari, Balusu and Digumarti Bhaskara Rao (1996). *Operation Black Board.* New Delhi : APH Publishing Corporation. ISBN 81-7024-711-X.

Veena Kumari, Balusu, Author and Digumarti Bhaskara Rao, Editor (2004). *Methods of Teaching Social Studies.* New Delhi : Discovery Publishing House. ISBN 81-7141-899-6.

Veena Kumari, Balusu, Author and Digumarti Bhaskara Rao, Editor (2000). *Psycho-Social Correlates of Achievement.* New Delhi : Discovery Publishing House. ISBN 81-7141-547-4.

Venkata Rao, B., Author and Digumarti Bhaskara Rao, Editor (2007). *Techniques of Teaching Chemistry.* New Delhi : Sonali Publications. ISBN 81-8411-057-X.

Venkata Rao, P. and Digumarti Bhaskara Rao (1989). *A Text Book of Zoology – Junior Intermediate.* Guntur : Vignan Publishers.

Venkata Rao, P. and Digumarti Bhaskara Rao (1989). *A Text Book of Zoology – Senior Intermediate.* Guntur : Vignan Publishers.

Venkateswara Rao, V., Author and Digumarti Bhaskara Rao, Editor (2004). *Problems of Education.* New Delhi : Discovery Publishing House. ISBN 81-7141-841-4.

Venkateswara Rao, V., V. Vijaya Lakshmi and V. Vamsi Krishna, Authors and Digumarti Bhaskara Rao, Editor (2004). *Education For All.* New Delhi : Sonali Publications. ISBN 81-88836-30-3.

Venkateswara Rao, V., V. Vijaya Lakshmi and V. Vamsi Krishna, Authors and Digumarti Bhaskara Rao, Editor (2004). *Education in India.* New Delhi : Sonali Publications. ISBN 81-88836-858-9.

Venkateswara Reddy, L. and Narayana, M. L, Authors and Digumarti Bhaskara Rao, Editor (2004). *Methods of Teaching Rural Sociology.* New Delhi : Discovery Publishing House. ISBN 81-7141-811-2.

Venkateswara Reddy, L. and Narayana, M. L., Authors and Digumarti Bhaskara Rao, Editor (2004). *Education for Dalits.* New Delhi : Discovery Publishing House. ISBN 81-7141-872-4.

Venkateswarlu, K. and S.J. Basha, Authors and Digumarti Bhaskara Rao, Editor (2004). *Methods of Teaching Commerce.* New Delhi : Discovery Publishing House. ISBN 81-7141-808-2.

Venugopala Rao, K., Author and Digumarti Bhaskara Rao, Editor (2000). *Teacher Morale in Secondary Schools.* New Delhi : Discovery Publishing House. ISBN 81-7141-551-2.

Venugopala Rao, K., Author and Digumarti Bhaskara Rao, Editor (2007). *Techniques of Teaching history.* New Delhi : Sonali Publications. ISBN 81-8411-059-6.

Vidya, C., Author and Digumarti Bhaskara Rao, Editor (1996). *A Text Book of Nutrition.* New Delhi : Discovery Publishing House. ISBN 81-7141-309-9.

Vijaya Bharathi, D., Author and Digumarti Bhaskara Rao, Editor (2000). *Educational Philosophies of Swami Vivekananda and John Dewey.* New Delhi : APH Publishing House. ISBN 81-7648-309-9.

Vijaya Bharathi, D., Author and Digumarti Bhaskara Rao, Editor (2005). *Educational Philosophy of John Dewey.* New Delhi : Discovery Publishing House. ISBN 81-8356-024-5.

Vijaya Bharathi, D., Author and Digumarti Bhaskara Rao, Editor (2005). *Educational Philosophy of Swami Vivekananda.* New Delhi : Discovery Publishing House. ISBN 81-8356-023-7.

Vijaya Kumar, S.J., Author and Digumarti Bhaskara Rao, Editor (2006). *Techniques of Teaching Mathematics.* New Delhi : Sonali Publications. ISBN 81-8411-039-1.

Vijaya Lakshmi, D., Author and Digumarti Bhaskara Rao, Editor (2004) *Basic Education.* New Delhi : Discovery Publishing House. ISBN 81-7141-881-3.

Vijaya Lakshmi, V., Author and Digumarti Bhaskara Rao, Editor (2006). *Techniques of Teaching Music.* New Delhi : Discovery Publishing House. ISBN 81-8411-038-3.

Vimala, T.D., B. Prasad Babu and Digumarti Bhaskara Rao, Editors (2007). *Stress, Coping and Management.* New Delhi : Sonali Publications. ISBN 81-8411-086-3.

Visalakshi, V., Author and Digumarti Bhaskara Rao, Editor (2006). *Techniques of Teaching Biology.* New Delhi : Sonali Publications. ISBN 81-8411-045-6.

Visalakshi, V., Author and Digumarti Bhaskara Rao, Editor (2007). *Techniques of Teaching Zoology.* New Delhi : Sonali Publications. ISBN 81-8411-055-3.

Index

L

M

N

O

P

Q

R

S